What We Do

Other Books by the author

I Had Every Intention
Dear All
Letters To A Middle Aged Poet
The Dust (10th anniversary edition)
Memoir And Essay
The Likes Of Us
Lost And Found
Careering Obloquy
Gorgeous Plunge
More Than All (with Ted Greenwald)
The Night Book
The River Road
Valu Pac
New York
The Blue Slope
Pantographic
96 Tears
Local Color/Eidetic Deniers

What We Do:

Essays for Poets

Michael Gottlieb

chax 2016

Trade Paperback Edition published by
Chax Press
PO Box 162
Victoria, TX 77902-0162

Chax Press is supported in part by the School of Arts & Sciences at the University of Houston-Victoria. We are located in the UHV Center for the Arts in downtown Victoria, Texas.

Chax acknowledges the support of graduate and undergraduate student interns and assistants who contribute to the books we publish.

This book is also supported by private donors. We are thankful to all of our contributors and members. Please see http://chax.org for more information.

Cover art:
Kirk Hayes
Ping Ping Ping, 2015
Oil on Panel (*trompe l'oeil*)
48 x 36 in (122 x 91 cm)
Courtesy of the artist and Zeiher Smith & Horton, New York
Photo: Matt Grubbs

Contents

Jobs of the Poets   7

Letters to a Middle-Aged Poet   51

A Spectre is Haunting the Poetry World   91

Author's Afterword   107

Jobs of the Poets

1.

We sit in our rooms. We write. We try to read. It begins to grow dark. We switch on the light. We wait for the world to come to us. Or, we don't. We start asking ourselves questions. Others arrive unbidden.

One of the questions: what kind of jobs do we, should we, as poets, end up with while we do our real job?

2.

What kind of job are poets 'allowed' to do? Academic? Starvation wage 'culture' jobs? Copy shop? Proofreading? Marrying for money? ...Trust fund poets (how many of them float around, incognito, clad in their carefully shabby protective coloration)?

And yet, nothing is better than this. Nothing is better than doing this – sitting up til all hours all alone, accompanied perhaps by ashtray and glass, listening to the trucks shudder up Lafayette or across Kenmare or along Amsterdam or the BQE or the Gowanus or...

So, naturally, we would prefer to do nothing else, wouldn't we? Even though, as Beerbohm rightly pointed out, you can't do this more than about an hour a day. So, is it that we take the path of least resistance? That is, 'I'll do whatever is least taxing so I can do what I really want,' or is it something else? Might it be that what we fear is really that 'something else?' That what we fear is that we cannot 'make it' in the world. The 'real world' – as we used to call it in college. Or, alternatively, is it that we just, quite properly, perhaps, recoil at the prospect of the demands, the compromises, the indignities, the surrenders that such a life appears to require?

So, how do we end up? Proofreading? Adjunct teaching? English As A Second Language? Construction? Bartending? Junior-assistant-odds-body? There was a time when some people got gigs writing pornography. You don't hear much about that anymore, probably because it was, in fact, pretty hard work. Some folks did typesetting, back when that was still a job. The apparent fact that these kinds of abnegation, this embrace of what some would call the 'menial' is a common or typical or credible option for us …what does that make us? Cleaner? Purer? Less compromised? But is that sort of work any less compromised than working for, say, the government or for a big company? How, by any law of political economy can that be so? What are we buying into, supporting? What's the difference? Or, is it just 'easier,' somehow, to have a crappy job? What do we trade off by not having to make any of those so-called trade-offs? Does one gain any more time for writing, or accumulate a stronger inclination to write, or a deeper aptitude for writing?

3.

What's wrong with working in a copy shop for twenty years, anyway?

Why is it, or is it, wrong to live like a graduate student? That is, like a slightly-well-off undergraduate - one step up from that especially luxurious poverty - for twenty years or more? Is it somehow wrong to camp out for decades in a cramped studio on Avenue C – back when that was the best address that a poet so situated could afford?

Moldering away there - crowded out by one's books and magazines, all stacked up on plank and cinderblock shelves - who have decided the place belongs to them? Why is – or is it ? – wrong not to have insurance? To always have to scrimp? Never taking a cab, always having to do your own laundry, never taking a vacation?

Not just hating what you do, but hating yourself for doing it? Never going out for a nice dinner in a decent restaurant in the West Village just because you feel like it, because it would mean a whole week's salary. To have to keep wearing every article of your clothing until it wears out. To look at everyone who walks in the door of the store who is dressed more expensively than you as someone who is somehow 'wrong.' Who is corrupt, or a fascist, or a potential criminal. What does it mean when you come to the pretty pass when you see any other way of living as a selling-out? And when you assume that every other life must be just as joyless as yours?

4.

Some would say things are different now.

No one can afford to live in, say, in New York, the way we did decades ago, some would say. The realities of the real estate market have changed all that. Poets have to have jobs now, real jobs, middle-class jobs. You just cannot live off a lousy job now, or a lousy part-time job. Poets can't afford to live out the old fantasy anymore.

Maybe people aren't working in copy shops anymore. But, for some people, nothing has changed. Aren't some people still making the same sort of portentous choices? Those first coming to the city? Those first launching themselves into this life? As opposed to those who have ten or twenty or thirty years invested in their choices and may naturally feel the need to defend them?

5.

Can it be, as is the opinion of some, that self-destructiveness is out of favor these days? That you can't show up falling down drunk at readings anymore? And, further, is it true, as some also aver, that most poets have decent jobs nowadays? Is this so, or is history repeating itself? In fact, is it possible that we really see, generation after generation, the same patterns occurring and reoccurring?

Are we all so well-behaved now? Is no one out of control anymore? Is no one getting fucked up anymore? Doesn't anyone grind up prescription pills anymore and share them round on a piece of mirror? Isn't anyone moving out of town, leaving New York, because they can't take it anymore? Does no one drop out so they can drink and play pool anymore? Is no one sitting at home with his or her kids in Brooklyn remembering bitterly all the years they ran a reading series and invited everyone on earth to read – and tediously conned up intro remarks for each and every one of them – and now no one, no one in the whole wide poetry world ever, ever calls on them? Does none of that befall anyone any longer?

6.

How or when or why has our job changed compared to the job of the painter, the artist (that is to say, why have we stayed so poor)?

Or was it always different – if so, why are there so many more of them? How has the art world become a phenomena in this apparently expanding, exploding universe of wealth? …In the same way, there used to be a handful of expensive restaurants in the city when we were young and now there are hundreds. Now there are hundreds of galleries in Chelsea when there used to be a few dozen in Soho a few decades ago and a mere dozen or so in Midtown a few decades before that. Now they are everywhere, the artists – compared to us. What does that say about us? That we seem to be so few and, moreover, that we are all staying poor, or relatively poor?

The idea that we are both really doing the same thing – but they can get rich doing it – and their old 'uns are given the Legion d'Honneur and ours the daily noodle special at Dojo – tells us exactly what? Does it tell us that there is something about us, or them, or what we respectively do, or, perhaps, the world itself that we all are obliged to live in? But we know it is the same. What we – the painters and the poets – *do* is the same. Is it that it is just too difficult, or too easy, to buy a poem?

7.

What were the prospects we thought we had before us in thirty years ago?

No one cared. But maybe that was just the way we were thinking three decades ago. What were we thinking? Some of us though, obviously, *were* thinking, and thinking ahead, in fact. The rest of us were just being poets, downtown poets, New York poets. We lived in that world, that small press, downtown reading scene-world. That was the scale and scope of our horizon. We didn't, we couldn't, and if anyone could possibly have asked, we would likely have responded that we *shouldn't* have had any greater ambition than that. No one wanted us anyway. No one from 'uptown,' no one from academia. They hated and disdained us. And certainly feared us. And that was all entirely proper and correct. Our painter and dancer and musician friends were in precisely the same boat.

We published each others poems. The Xeroxed books at first – it wasn't so long since mimeo had ruled the day. Some of us had special staplers that could do saddle stapling, but not many. They were expensive. Some of us had IBM Selectrics, but even fewer. They were extremely expensive.

There was a remaindered paper dealer on Broadway, below Houston, behind a Latin women's wear retailer named Yo Linda! You could go back there and find cheap card stock for covers and lovely sheets of tissue in all sorts of colors for end papers. I always assumed they once owned the building, or at least the lease on the ground floor. And, like a squabbling brood of Czarist nobles crowded after the Revolution into the butler's pantry of the mansion they'd once owned, they'd been progressively reduced, stacking their teetering piles of stock at the back of the ground floor where we came to roam. There's a Banana Republic there now.

8.

How has that changed for the second, third, fourth generations?

Somehow – how? But we know exactly how, don't we? Somehow, in a way that seemed impossible for us back then, or all wrong - that tenured, or, at least adjunct, lifestyle – one which it seemed ridiculous for the likes of us back then to even countenance, somehow that lifestyle now has become normative, normal. And why? How could this have come to pass? And at what cost?

9.

Is obscurity good for poets? That is, why must we remain unacknowledged legislators?

Are we not most at home when alone in a crowd? Might it be better to pass along Fourth Avenue unnoticed? To walk among our fellows on the pavement in front of the Strand, as if we were no different than them, because, after all, we are not. To listen and to look unhindered, unrecognized, does that not give us the greatest agency, freedom, that any artist could ask for? We are <u>just</u> like everyone else – we should be, we have to be, we should be proud to be so. We just do one other thing – one thing in addition, one thing different than everyone else. The fact that no one pays the slightest attention to us only redounds to our benefit. It permits us to do our job better, easier.

And how much more obscure would we all be if some of us had not become academics and so made sure that at least someone is reading some of our books, year after year?

10.

Is the academic lifestyle healthy for poets?

So, in a way that frankly was completely unthinkable thirty years ago, at least to many, if not most of us, somehow this came to pass. Where and how were the seeds of this transformation embedded in our original, critical, valorized proposition? Now this tenured life is a normal way for poets like us to live. But what is that life like? What are the pressures? Are they more or less than any other job? And what about mobility? Does this profession give one more, less, or the same amount of freedom to maneuver, to move around, than other possible ways of making a living? And what is the ease, or lack thereof, when it comes to moving from stage to stage, or level to level in that world, compared to any other? How important is that anyway? Trapped? Are we not all trapped? Or, are we all equally trapped?

And does it pay more? Well, we know it pays more than working in the copy shop. At least it does eventually. And, lastly, is that world more or less hierarchical or stratified than others? Does it require the same or less amount of obeisance? Does it oblige its denizens to acknowledge designations of rank, status, title and perquisite more than other ways of making a living?

11.

Is the 'business' world worse?

Is any other world less hierarchical than academia? Less mobile?
With more pressure to conform? Or, are they all equally oppressive?
One can answer what one will to those questions but behind them
is another question: how much more morally compromised is the
business world for example, bearing in mind how it is linked, however,
to the profit motive, to the corruption and evil of capitalism? How
much more is it connected to some more or less base dimension of
commerce, of deception, of filthy lucre? And, if so, how much more
corrupt is that life than an academic life whose economy is itself as we
know, a vast dependency upon the largesse of the State – regardless
whether the institution in question is a public or a private one. Do not
all colleges and universities, by virtue of their utter dependency upon
grants and other public funding, therefore become instrumentalities,
both economically and morally, of the state? And for those whose
endowments libeate them from that dependency, where and how are
those endowments invested?

What does that leave us with? Teaching as an intrinsically ethical
activity? Let us stipulate to that. But what does that say about all the
other pursuits we could follow, all the other things we could spend our
days doing? Working in a copy shop on Seventh Avenue, or working
in an agency on Madison Ave? Providing a good or a service to others?
Working for some non-profit on Park Avenue South and accepting

the delimiting compromises that demands – those bien pensant indignities? Or, one of those dead-end jobs at a trade publisher, with its veneer of culture and decorum and its false-front of non-commercial security – but even more boldly underpaying? What are the ethical dimensions of what you spend your day doing?

12.

Is the academic lifestyle so much more 'congenial' for writing, for poetry?

How many of us really want to be teaching? Would any of us have become teachers if we weren't poets? Is it that that lifestyle seems to 'allow' the most time, for poetry? How many, as some occasionally ask, enjoy having what passes for the power over others that a teacher wields over a student? But – if there was another, equally renumerative path, apparently equally undemanding, equally morally comfortable – would we take that instead? Or, is it that we are also frightened (not just repelled) by the 'real' world? The business world? Do we fear that we could never survive there?

13.

So, what is the difference between working in a copy shop and an English Dept? Is it not possible that both are equally 'relieving' of responsibility and both equally, safely, ineluctably, distant from the life of the writing mind?

That drafty, sooty shop on St. Marks or Eighth Street or Broome Street or First Avenue or Sixth Avenue, with its soiled matte white paint and jerry rigged carpentry, its awkward, amateurish signage; its tired equipment and bickering staff. The ugly looks that fall like rain on the boss whenever he chances to fall by, the petty pilferage. The anger that just continues to build…

14.

Or, could some argue the English Department life is, really, after all, more conducive, more sympathetic for a poet? That the fight over the corner office, for the department secretary's hours, for the next sabbatical – that is all good. It engenders, indeed, it furthers our project.

But if we end up saying that writing is indeed as distant from teaching as is working in a copy shop, why pick one over another? Because teaching offers better pay and benefits and a sabbatical? The impact of those facts certainly cannot be underestimated. They are vital for the sustenance of our mind's life. That sounds like reason enough. But are there any other reasons? Or, alternatively, could it be that there are reasons that would make a life in a copy shop superior, more conducive, more sympathetic, more ameliorative for the life of a poet? Is it possible that life in the English Department in fact forces compromises upon one that spending eight hours a day bent over a Xerox machine does not?

In academia, might there more pressure to conform, for example? Pressure, specifically, to ensure that one's writing aligns with the aesthetics and literary politics of those – to conjure a wildly hypothetical example – who are in a position to do one a good turn or do one ill; say, the head of one's department or those who have a say in one's future, when it comes to writing recommendations, or the granting of tenure?

15.

Why shouldn't poets be the free-est of all artists? Freed from any economy, freer than any to do whatever they wish? No capital, no infrastructure, no collaboration required?

What is holding us back? There's no money in this anyway. And no one else cares, anyway. To the extent that we are actually unlettered, untethered - except possibly if we claim we are academics, and our work, as poets, our lives as poets, have no relationship whatsoever to what puts our bread on the table, because that is simply a fact for so many of us – it should follow, perforce, that if our only responsibilities are to ourselves, and each other – as defined as those who are with us now, readers as well as writers, and those who have come before and those who will follow - why, by all that we hold dear, are we not the most free?

So, one might ask, why does there appear to be more conformity now in our world than there was, say, twenty or thirty years ago? When the Gotham was still on 47th Street, when it was still open, and there were just one or two magazines to be found there with anything in them along the lines of what we'd today recognize as the product of 'us.' That is to say, are poets more in lock step? More attentive to how they are different rather than how they are the same? If that is so, can that be simply due to what we can call a 'maturing model' that our type of writing somehow has found itself tracking? That at this stage a refining or winnowing away has already taken place?

Perhaps it is 'our' problem – as in 'us,' the older poets. Perhaps we have been around too long and we are no longer capable of reading the way we used to. We cannot perceive the real differences, the actual variety. Could it be that it all may so often seem of a piece to us because our eyes have grown dull? In the same way, that, to some, all the rock and roll produced after their own particular youth has come to a close, which is when they themselves stopped listening closely, starts to sound quite the same?

Or, are our expectations all wrong? How many of us – that same 'us' referred to above – somehow find ourselves wishing for some cataclysm, some violent overthrow, some one or some group to come along and definitively reject us? Some 'next?' Some clear and definitive full-stop? Something to come along that will be so new that it will sweep us aside? We have had our day, haven't we? It is as if our ultimate validation, as a movement, as a school, as individual artists even, perhaps, can only come from our passing.

Alternatively, to return to the present, to the here-and-now, to the situation in which we find ourselves and which many would say in which we've been immured for perhaps a couple of decades - if there is indeed some more uniformity in what we read, is it possible that it is due to the fact that so much of what people are reading, when they come upon this writing, is presented in a classroom setting, in the form of a syllabus? And, if so, it is a reading list selected by ....who? Is it also possible that, further, as these young 'uns begin to write, so much of the criticism and response they receive is modulated in the venue of a credit-bearing writing workshop led by... who? Who among our peers or those who have come immediately after us and who may be tenured or themselves strive for that rank?

16.

What does it mean to be so free that one has no audience save other poets?

Does it matter who we write for? An audience that is not here yet? An audience that never will be? An audience that is dead, living, yet-to-be-born? Do we write for an idea, not an ideal, but an idea of an audience? Because musn't poetry be written for all of us, including those who ignore or refute or spurn us and our activity? Like, for example, those who used to venture into the bars where we used to read, like the Ear Inn, looking for a game on the TV, and retreat, smirking when they realized what they had blundered into. So that we, all of us, can be what we *have* to be. We, ourselves, are as good an audience as any. For the time being, at least. Maybe forever. And why shouldn't we be?

17.

If communitarianism is what we like to believe is the equivalent of a market in this poetry world, its currency is, what, exactly? Interaction? Readings? Publishing events?

So, what kind of world have we created in lieu of the kind of world that our cousins, the artists, live in, only a scant few blocks away, over in Chelsea? What kind of cashless economy is this? Let us put aside the academic economy and its near-relative, the world of grants and residencies, prizes and the like. What then are we seeking to delineate here? What is the question we are trying to answer? *Is* there an economy? And, if so, how is it denominated? But is that even first question we should be asking? Is there something more we are missing by asking the questions in this way? What, in the final respect, is the nature of our organization? Who are we, when we are seen in company, in sum? Is this a community at all? And, if so, how are we organized, how do we communicate with ourselves, how do we *work?*

18.

What is the myth that causes us to fear the real world so? The myth that has us assume that we can't cope? That the best of all possible worlds is the one in which we can write all day... and not cope? To not have to deal with the 'real world' ...at all, or hardly at all. That it is okay to have a crappy job... so that, for decades, we will be sure to have 'enough' time to write...

Are we so much better than the world around us, this corrupt, grubby world? This world where we try to avoid getting run over by black SUVs ferrying around morons wearing suits that cost more than we make in a month. Must we avoid inveigling ourselves in that kind of corruption? That world of compromise? Are we afraid? Afraid that we might not have the skills, or ability to compete with those we feel are not our equals? Is it competition itself?

So, when we say we cannot deal with the 'politics' of a place, a workplace, say – what are we saying? That we can't deal with the duplicity or the shifting terms and conditions of the place or, is it that we fear that we just can't interact with others on that level of complexity? We can't or don't want to have to put that much time and energy into that sort of thing, into having to deal with others? Do we think that we can't deal with this? Don't want to? Shouldn't have to? Are we too good for all of that or do we really think that we aren't good enough?

19.

Which leads to that retreat. That stepping back. That consolation which writing provides. This is something we are good at. Which no one can take away. Which leads to other problems, all too often.

If we are most alive when we are writing, if we can sit and say to ourselves, this is what we are here for, this is why we are, say, placed upon this earth, to do this work, when I am doing this I am making use of all of my faculties, all of my powers, I am on fire, I am finally alive, here doing what I was put on earth to do, in this room, in this apartment in this corner of Kings County, if this what I am meant to do then everything that I have done, read, trained myself toward has led me to this very moment. When I sit and write, and do this work which the world needs so badly, which no one else in the world can do, why is it so much better to do it with the aid of some sort of stimulant? Or is it? What drives so many of us, or some of us, or perhaps all of us to, to say we need to put something extra in our bodies when we sit down to work?

Is it that we are just trying to heighten our powers, increase our ability to focus, to apply ourselves? To facilitate the flow, to free or unblock or engage or disengage, is that why we do, or did, put those things in our bodies? Alternatively, if writing gives us so much pleasure sober or straight, how much more pleasure, or so the argument could go, can it give us with the aid of one or another sort of substance?

Or, could it be that there might be some correlation between this writing, and its ability to enable us to block out the very world that we are trying to 'reach?' And could that such 'blocking out' is instrumental to the activity itself? We need to 'blot out' the world in order to save it? That is, to focus in upon it. And that selfsame fear that says that, pace above, we cannot deal with so many dimensions of the real world, like having a real job, conspires to turn poetry into a retreat, a shelter. Do we write poems because we don't or can't do those other things? And, by extension when we sit and drink or smoke or do other things might it not be that we are in fact retreating further?

But what about that veritable, undeniable flush of wellbeing, the racing of the pulse that the act of writing produces, and which writing itself may very well be intended to produce. The pleasure of it.

And abandon? …What about Abandon's vital, historical, central role in our activity? Its honored place in our profession's armamentarium? If one stipulates that part of our job is in fact to look upon this world from a certain distance and cast it in a new light, can not one also argue that such work requires a degree of untethering, of unshackling? And some vehicle of abandon – somehow or anyhow achieved is, in or of itself, required? How we achieve same, then, can be said to beg the question. We cannot always be sober, can we?

The poets have their gods and their lights, and their honored traditions. The fruits of the vine, for example, are said to be counted among them. And, we can aver, so have they forever been. And forever shall. But so is, and was, and likely will be - alcoholism, and the other addictions.

20.

Sensation and abandon

Nonetheless, can it be that it is in our interest to embrace abandon more than others, than those so-called 'civilians,' say? Because we are that much more in the throes of 'sensation.' That is, is it because we 'feel' so much, and therefore we are then so much more sensitive, that we need to free, lose, anesthetize ourselves so much more than people who aren't so... so what? ...tuned in, perhaps, or receptive, or creative? Can any of us actually mouth such a line with a straight face? How much bad behavior has been excused under this tattered rag of what passes for argument?

21.

To what degree should this indulgence, this 'gimme,' this lifestyle Mulligan,
apply for everyone, not just poets – everyone who has or has to have a job?
And then, who does that exclude?

If we have an inalienable right to pursue Abandon (and who doesn't)
who should be excluded from the class of creative types? Or, who
are those who are under or so much pressure from the constraints
or contradictions inherent in the way they have to live that they
might not also have the same right to lose themselves… to embrace
irresponsibility? Who, in other words, doesn't get a free pass… to mess
up, to get messed up, to wake us up as they kick over garbage cans and
throw up into the gutter on Essex St.?

22.

There is an eternal war against laziness, forever being lost.

There seems to be a relationship between sloth and creation. There is the allure, and virtue, of entropy. Of course, many would argue that the cousin of abandon is indeed sloth, as the cousin of application is obsession. Obsession manifests itself in a phenomenon of which we are all too familiar in our world: writing *too* much. And how vital, ever-present is sloth in how we define ourselves? Not only as a badge of honor particular to our calling, with a long and honorable role in our history, but also might it not have a more central role, as the noble Max B famously remarked (more fully cited below)? Could it be that some of this sort of 'time' is necessary, for us to spend, to expend? So that we can properly execute our role in life?

If that is in fact the case, might that then go to the argument that the copy-shop on Bleecker Street lifestyle, e.g. the "mental-sloth enabling" lifestyle, that is to say the entirely unchallenging life style might in the final respect prove to be a rational, appropriate, altogether proper choice for at least some of us?

23.

Should it not therefore be so much easier to be a poet than, say, a painter? If part or all of our argument is that we are men, or women, essentially like every other man or woman – seeing the world and reacting thusly, when we make or create what we do, does it not make it simpler, and cleaner, and more appropriate that in every way except in the act of making what we make, we are indeed just like everyone else?

Why do we think we should be held up for approbation because of this one thing – no matter how heroic we believe it is? Or perhaps does it in fact not make us different or better than anyone else at all?

And, does not our obscurity oblige us to live in two worlds – separate but related, in a way that many of our peers, say, in the art world do not? They may not be obliged to deal with these issues. We walk the streets of that other world, the every day world of regular men and women. Unseen, unrecognized. It makes it easier to suss it all out, does it not? It is the source, after all, and destination of our work, is it not? We live in that world, the world of grimy sneaker stores on Broadway, and yet we do not.

As artists we can dwell in it – that world, this world, and we must, with a thoroughgoingness that others can't - because we have no options. We are obliged to live this greater, or *worser,* one. And, in theory at least, we can pass with the greatest fluidity and return to our other world, the one in which our art lives, and reigns.

24.

But, we do know, we feel it in our bones, that creating, that being a maker, is in fact the highest form of being. We just know it. That is why we know that we are most alive, most human - perhaps the only time we are fully alive - when we are engaged in this work.

At the same time we must remind ourselves that we are no better, in any way, than the next man, the next woman. That the utility of our role is no more central to our species than any other. Yet, we know that what we do is so important that the world depends upon us, even though it thinks it can ignore us. But no definition of humanity can be deemed complete without us. It doesn't matter if no one reads us except us.

25.

What about our 'non-poetry' responsibilities? Is there some voice telling us, some overtone in the conversation hinting, some knot in the fabric of the mantle that we are presented with, or which we see ourselves donning when we decide that this is the life we want to live, that tells us that it is alright to oblige them — any of them, all of them — to take the back seat? Our lovers, spouses, children, our siblings, our parents?

Is our calling so high that it absolves us of all other or most or some other responsibilities? To others? To ourselves? Or, can it be that such a definition of this calling, this responsibility can turn into an excuse, a refuge, a retreat, a shell that we can crawl into? Does this vocation excuse all?

What right do we have to relegate anyone else to second class citizenship? Who are we to say that our ability to do our job — being a poet, that is, is so important that the happiness or wellbeing of anyone around us, to the extent that we can affect it, is of lesser importance?

Or, by the same token, what does it mean if you are sitting at the front of a classroom or at the head of the table in a big conference room and suddenly it hits you, as it does with shockingly unremitting force each time, that what you do for a living has nothing whatsoever to do with what you really believe you are all about?

26.

What does it mean to shrink, to abandon, to refuse them? That is, those to whom we could or should be responsible, and do so in the name of poetry? For the sake of poetry, and its own responsibilities? What does that say about us, about any privileged claims that our poetry might make? What is the moral foundation for valorizing poetic activity in such a way that such a position seeks to justify all manner of bad behavior?

Do we have any right? Does it not erode any claim we can make for our work or ourselves? Or, are we outside the law, any laws, any rules? Does that mean, if so, that we should feel free to screw each other over as freely and with as little compunction as that world, which so many of us condemn as corrupt, screws over us?

27.

What are we here for, anyway?

To have the good time which others can't? To stay at the Ukrainian Bar, the St. Marks Bar and Grill, the Red Bar, the Spring Lounge later than anyone else? And if that is their job, if their job is to have that good time, what happens if they can't remember it? Or, if they can remember it, what happens if they can't describe it aright? Is that it? Is that all? Or, perhaps, is it something else? Could it be that we are here to help? Do we have any sort of responsibility? To help people through the day? To make some things easier for people, to make some things harder? To make some things easier to forget, some things impossible to forget? Might we have a job to do?

28.

Do our responsibilities just extend to other poets? That is, to our peers, to poets of the past, to poets of the future? And to readers too? Do we have responsibilities to other others? E.g. what are our responsibilities not as poets firstly, or solely, but as adults, as members of families, as friends, as citizens, as neighbors, as fellows of the same community, to the others to whom we are connected, however denominated? And how do we reconcile these different responsibilities? Can we?

Does the nature of our work as poets, as artists, absolve us of all other responsibility? Is this work so hard, of such a high calling, that we should not be burdened with other responsibilities? Does it mean that we have every right to get high in the middle of the day? Or short of that, every night? Does what we think of our ability to see into the heart of things, and other people, mean that the rules which others must abide by should not apply to us? Are we better than those people? If not, what does that say about our work? That is, is it possible that our <u>work</u> is not necessarily more important than anyone else's? Say, a collection agent's or a bond salesman's? But how can that be?

29.

When it comes to discharging our responsibilities, in the first instance –
those writing-related ones, whatever we decide they are, or indeed, in the
second, the ones that don't seem to have anything to do with our writing,
whichever among those we decide to recognize or accept, if any; as difficult
as it can seem to carry on shouldering them, or some of them or any of them
during the best of times, or during times which we can look back at later and
deem to be uneventful ...that is to say, no matter how difficult it can seem to
carry on simply in the face of the everyday conditions one seems obliged to
accept, what happens when something really terrible happens?

When some event, however defined, befalls one, what then? The kind
of every-day horror, or tragedy, that we must admit are part and parcel,
eventually, of virtually everyone's life? People get sick. People die. They
die before they are supposed to. People fall in front of the Number 3
train. Terrible things happen. Does being a poet help one to carry on
when caught in the meshes of the Other? Does exhibiting what we
presume to be uncompromising honesty along with the requirement to
see what stands before us in all its detail or horror without any illusion
whatsoever, in other words, those vital aspects what we think of as
our job description as poets – does any of this stand us in good stead,
armor us at all in times of need. Can it?

Or, do we fall apart just as easily? Is our ability to cope, or not, with
loss or tragedy or the like, if cope is the right word, based upon certain
qualities or facilities that are entirely independent of whatever skills

or qualities we have or have developed that have made us the poets or artists that we like to think we are?

Nevertheless, might it not be that those accelerating tempos of threat, those shaking echoes of loss, those vertiginous gusts of terror and false-respite, no matter however temporary, that are so often the orchestration of crisis and disaster, like a terminal illness for example, which we can see, we cannot help but see, all follow a particular, perhaps choreographed structure, an outline, some sort of intrinsic teleology that somehow — since, after all, it is no small part of our role to see pattern everywhere no matter how fugitive, whether on the page or in a ward at Bellevue — perhaps makes that very inability on our part to surmount or navigate those horrors with any more success or equanimity or aplomb or whatever than any other group or type, all the sadder, pathetic, tragic... that makes it even clearer how much like, and no better, we are than any other group of humanity under the sun?

And, by the same token — does what we do, what we make — does any of that help those who read our poems? Can we help? Do we make a difference? Are we useful? Must we not tell ourselves that it is so? And is it not?

30.

There is our 'everyday' and then there is our horror, our crisis. And then, over there, there are other people whose 'everyday' may very well represent what is, to us, the most terrible of outcomes possible, the most horrible of lives. For example, what about the person who every day goes to a job that he or she hates, just for the sake of someone else? Or, for the sake of being able to do, when the workday is done... being able to do something else?

This is the reverse of abandon. This is focus to end all. So, what about *that* person? E.g. if we say our 'highest duty' as artists is to serve others, what about those, those people whose explicit day-to-day lives - that is to say, their jobs are exactly so defined to put food on their family's tables and nothing else. What does it mean if that in order for them to do that they are obliged to engage in work that they despise? How is that like or unlike our situation: what we are, in the final respect, so lucky to be able to engage in is work that, despite all the black obscurity it immures us in, devolves terrific pleasure and joy upon us. What if in fact that other, duty-bound, work we have to take on in order to do our writing, is work that we hate? If we hate having to do it, day after day, year after year? But we continue to do it. For others? For the sake of others? Is that heroic? But, how it is that we so confidently say, if only to ourselves, as we swagger about, and, we do, don't we, that we are then superior in some sort of way to those souls, sweeping floors or making someone else's beds at the Comfort Inn, even, say, repossessing someone else's car on Jerome Avenue – when they are doing exactly what we are doing? They are doing some work they very well may hate, but continue doing for the sake of others.

31.

We too are a service industry.

32.

As Max Beerbohm said, "the only problem with being a poet is figuring out what to do with the other twenty-three hours of the day."

Letters to a Middle-Aged Poet

1.

So, what did you expect?

2.

What does it mean when you, who putatively were thinking life-and-death thoughts all along, you are a poet after all, aren't you, get faced with some life-and-death-related realities, or rather, some specifically death-related realities, of your own?

You too. And it is you lying there waiting for the surgeon. But first the anesthesiologist, as in the proper order of things, comes to you and gives you his talk, practiced, with all the due diligence and nods to your involvement, your intellectual engagement, however specious, as part of the so-called process; his weary and not altogether tolerant acceptance of your small-talk, his grudging acknowledgement of your pallidly irreverent jokes.

As he continues, spinning out his practiced lines: what to expect, what else can go wrong, as if you weren't already aware, as if there weren't enough things already that could go wrong… you can see in his eyes, unrolling in a kind of practiced unspoken declamation, an array of additional terms and conditions. It is a demarche. In no uncertain terms he is demanding you acknowledge that what you have been offering up are no more than feeble sallies, proxies, actually – less than proxies, stand-ins for proxies – that's what they are, nothing like any real challenge to him and all of his kind – to all of their utter sway over you; their sovereign, regnant power over your body, your fate, and those who are there to stand with you this day.

3.

Assuming that we wake up and then come back to earth and eventually return to circulation, an unexpected question arises as one realizes that one is not a ghost, not invisible, in fact apparently as corporeal or at least as noticeable as one was before, at least as much as anyone else, apparently, in the immediate vicinity: when it comes those in the room who still pay us any attention, why do any of them bother?

Out of respect, or due diligence, or due diffidence or because, in fact, they remain interested in something, anything, we might still be able to offer up?

Is it obligation? Does it arise out of something that we did, we accomplished, we created, something or other we are or were responsible for, however many years ago; something perhaps that is over and done with? Is that why you all are paying attendance upon us, upon 'me,' whomever 'me' mayhap be defined as, for the purposes of this activity?

4.

But then what happens when, as will inevitably befall us all, as poets, should we live long enough, some come along who deign to supersede us; some who, we should be so lucky, acknowledge us, not ungenerously grant us our due and then calmly let us know that they are moving on?

Us, superseded. Us, a great deal of whose claim to fame was our decisive and dramatic rejection of all or, rather, of so much of what had come before us.

They have left us behind. They have taken off from our innovations, our revolutionary changes, our decisive moments – obviously they are beyond us now – and have hove off into the future. Where does that leave us? We were supposed to be the future.

However, truth be told, how long were we waiting for something else to come along, to succeed us, to move beyond us? For *that* quite possibly came to seen as the truest sort of validation our own project, since it would serve to confirm that the radicalism of what we were doing could not, in the long run, be institutionalized, but only digested and then subsumed.

So now they're telling us, 'thanks and we'll take it from here.'

5.

What are we supposed to do now?

Do we try and hop about those fast-moving freights? Do we claim that we too are one of them, that we are card carrying members of their movements – we're with them and just like them – and always have been (even before they were conceived of), or does that make us seem ridiculous? And, if we do not try and sport those onsies or romper suits or ill-fitting skinny jeans or (for those of us capable of sprouting same) that artfully curated facial hair – what indeed is left for us?

If we can't be one of them, can't carry that off, are we obliged to ask ourselves: why bother writing at all anymore?

6.

What if our reaction to all that is going on around us is not some cringe-worthy, pathetic attempt to climb aboard an express that has left the station several decades after we had our own tickets once and forever punched, but, instead, something else?

Perhaps our posture should be one of welcoming. Maybe we should be able to get it together to write some positive criticism, a supportive review or two. We could even assume, or presume, the mantle of a champion. Let's not dismiss such a possibility out of hand. But what if the reaction, our reaction, is different? Speciously curmudgeonly? Angry, vexatious, rejectionist? What if our response is a frankly hostile, knee-jerk dismissal of whatever it is that naturally – some might say – quite naturally, comes after what we ourselves in our youth, in our own day, served up to the world?

7.

If the shoe doesn't fit, must you find someone to throw it at?

There are so many ways to go. Ways to go wrong, to go crazy, to go off the rails. Ways to go quietly. Not so quietly.

Which is worse? Trying to hop aboard that train that is leaving without you – because all of the riders are twenty or thirty or even forty years than you, and, even if you had some hand in designing the locomotive or mapping the train's route, lo how many years ago, this train is not one you hold a ticket for, or have any reason to be riding; or, on the other hand, let us say you have no interest whatsoever in riding that on line… what does it mean when you damn with faint praise, or just plain damn everything that's come along after you?

"It's all just a faint echo of what we did years ago." "It's fake." "It's empty." "It's shallow." "It's playing tennis without a net." "It's not about anything." "It's a pose. They're all poseurs."

Doesn't sound a lot like what was once said about us?

At the heart of it all is it an inability to come to grips with, to accept, one's own place? One's place, inside of time? Our day may be done; or it may not. We may have been superseded, or not. But the fact is that these are indeed our children. Our kids – and we, the fact is, we are kids no more.

8.

*What do you do when you suspect, you fear, that you have nothing new –
despite everything, absolutely everything you are doing, trying, attempting,
as you strive to strike off in a novel direction – nothing new at all to say?*

What are you to do when you see others, those inevitably younger,
so much younger than you, effortlessly executing, working, exploring,
gamboling in areas, in regions that you know – as soon you come
across their latest – that you can never, will never, in fact, should never
yourself even try to venture to? What do you do now?

Do you stop? Is it now time to accept that your day is done and
whatever you had to contribute, you've already gone ahead and given at
the office? On the other hand, can the example of those others, those
young 'uns, perhaps prompt us, prod us, push us into new areas, into
new ways of thinking about our own work, our selves, our joint and
several, our shared, and our – alternatively – our severed worlds? New
thinking which will oblige us, impel us to do something different?

The snap-brim fedora is not for us, nor those tight selvage dungarees,
rolled up at the ankle, nor the brogues without socks, much less the
ornate mustachios, nor the midriff baring outfits – but we cannot, we
should not carry on as if we were unaware that they have come, or
have come again, to have their day, their hour upon the stage. To say
this is not to suggest what our younger colleagues are engaged in is
mere fashion. It is just to argue that it is so far, *that* far from us; and

we need, we must, in our own interest as well as theirs, I would suggest – necessarily – acknowledge that distance, that difference. We must so stipulate.

Elsewise, if we cannot somehow accept them then there seems to be nothing else to do except *stop*. And to stop and fix one's gaze on the past – not in order to understand it or try and reuse it but, instead to do a header into it and live there, because everything else, everything since then, does not… cannot… satisfy, and is simply, irreducibly, irrevocably, a recipe for self-immolation.

9.

Do the dangers of repeating oneself include more than just reusing themes or styles, line-breaks or indentations?

Didn't I use that word before, in 1979 or 1986, in 2003? But – how do I check, without rereading everything all over again?

I mean *individual* words. And, not words like 'like' but like 'suppurating' or 'decorticating' …the sort of words which, because of the weight which they are asked to bear, or perhaps because of the weight which you, which I, which we – as poets, have chosen to pile upon their shoulders, if one ends up using them over and over, or even more than once, one ends up looking like…. what? Foolish? Inattentive? Ineffectually, impotently repetitive? Why else would you repeat yourself unless you had nothing new to say?

10.

What is the contour, the profile, the outline, the model of the life we've chosen?

Are we all one-trick-ponies, lucky enough when we are, or, rather when we were young enough to have managed to accomplish whatever it was we set out to achieve? And further, is it the nature of our activity, our profession, that we can never, should never expect to repeat that? That is, must we submit to the dictum that we each have had our own particular moment, one moment when we were in touch – in touch with something – and we should be grateful for that? Is this, in the final reckoning, a young person's game? Or, is it one that follows some ineluctable arc? An arc which may achieve its zenith sooner or perhaps a bit later but, whether that high-point occurs in one's twenties or thirties or even forties, at some point – and definitely we're past that point – must we accept that we are on the downhill slope?

Alternatively, might this indeed be, in fact, a life-long project, one that entails, that requires, that promises a life-long engagement – with the world, with poetry, with those who came before us, with those we came up with as well as those who came after us, as well as, well, ourselves? Is this a life which holds the promise, possibly, maybe, just maybe of change and transformation and the long-term possibility of value, of 'relevancy' (whatever that means) and of some sort of, dare we say, redemption? Is any of that real, possible, not absurdly banal?

11.

Seizing upon. Seizing up.

What happens, as it seems to so often, increasingly often, amongst us at this age, when we spring upon an idea, an idée, an idée fixe and don't let go?

The way it, the lovely idée itself, explains everything. The way it can grow, take up whatever shape the moment or argument requires, shape-shift to accommodate all – and every – manner of situation. So elegant, so simple yet so expansive. The way it *solves* everything. It must. It has to. And it does so, so effortlessly. Is it because we've grown tired of 'looking' …or, as always, are we afraid of sliding into irrelevancy?

It is not just an organizing principle. It is a lens, a filter, is it not? A new first principle, a call-to-action, through which the world, whichever world is the general focus, if not the world in the widest sense, the broadest definition of all, is now forever to be organized.

The saddest part of these fixations, when one finds them in those no-longer-young, is that unlike what ensues when they manifest themselves in the young, for whom hope always abides that they, the individuals in question, will indeed grow out of them, there is the sinking realization when we see this malady strike our peers that it may indeed, in fact quite probably will, turn out to be a permanent condition.

Fine, we can say: let anyone believe what they will. What is wrong with that? What could possibly be wrong? This is Liberty Hall, is it not? What can possibly go wrong? Nothing of course. Nothing at all. It matters not at all, or perhaps not too much, if these constructs, these models, these armatures are themselves specious or superficial or our friends mount their private rostrums and begin enunciating their particular, particularized, personalized rhetoric. We cannot help but see Polonius before us. Garbed in contemporary rags, or perhaps the wide-wale corduroy or the faded denim of a few decades past, but it is we see Polonius before us, nonetheless, gesticulating meaningly. It matters not much at all, and certainly he, or she, is harmless. Or not?

But what happens when something or someone comes along which or who refuses to fit into the prescribed model? Someone who refuses to accept its or his or her pre-determined role, who so clearly rejects the basic assumptions upon which our idée is founded, upon which it altogether depends, and does so, invariably, in that insouciantly ignorant way the young always seem to call up, in a way that seems of second nature to them. And then what happens? What happens when those young 'uns refuse to fit into the neat boxes we've reserved for them? Rage? Elder-rage? After all, we are not young. Pounding on the worn Formica in the tired coffee shop? The suddenly anxious waiter hovering at a distance?

What is to become of us, of those of us in such thrall... what happens then?

12.

This isn't over.

Is it?

How much of what might be called the anger or the confusion or the rejection, plain and simple – rejection of what's arrived lately – that arises amongst those of a certain age, might not really be a product of principled or even unprincipled aesthetic or ideological objections but instead, to put it bluntly, might in fact based on the simple, sinking realization that one is becoming irrelevant, or indeed, invisible in *other* ways?

Of all these young ones, some of them, needless to say, needs be deemed attractive – there are enough of them that the odds augur so – are there not? That only stands to reason. Others are comely in a way that we see now, now that we are old enough, by virtue of what is no more than a concomitant component of their youth, a quality inherent in them all, at least to some degree, at least for a time. They seem pretty to us just because they are young.

While it very well may be that not only have they have no need of your poems – at least no longer – the fact is, it is likely that they don't want or need you, yourself, in any amatory or physical way anymore either. Not even in a theoretical or – how to put it? – statistically significant way. You have nothing left to offer. And so, how much of the anger arising among us, directed at them, might very well might flow from that fact, wittingly grasped by us or not?

13.

In the end, why do we keep on?

To what degree did we say to ourselves when we were young that this activity might somehow not just bestow some otherwise unobtainable value on our lives, or even in some way ennoble us, but in addition, by virtue of the possibility that our work could – in theory, at least – abide after we ourselves had departed from this plane, this earth, could in fact – notwithstanding how fantastic a notion, not to mention infantile, if not downright pathetic, such conjuring may indeed seem to us now – provide us with, at least for a few years, some period of, let's call it, a life-after-life?

And, truth be told, to what degree might that have been an impulse, a driver impelling us on? And, if so, now that we are so much closer to that inevitable expiry date, how are we obliged, if at all, to rethink that proposition?

Now that we see how quickly and completely so many of our friends and peers unfairly and cruelly have been cut from our ranks at an untimely age, and are already well on the way – if they are not there already – to oblivion… who speaks of them, those among us who are gone already? Who speaks for them? Who speaks up for them?

And we won't likely be able to dodge this particular reckoning either, surely. Those dread, fell, inconsolable, overmastering premonitions that grip us – and who among us has not felt them – each and every time one ventures into a bookstore, any bookstore… into for example, the nether reaches of the Strand with its mile upon mile of sad, soiled, largely forgotten hard-backed tomes, the works of thousands upon thousands of once proud and strutting authors, now largely consigned to oblivion. And what are we, compared to them?

14.

How much of what's gone wrong in our lives do we ascribe to either the quotidian vicissitudes that could and do befall any – and so many – of us or, alternatively... do we as poets, because we are poets, do we say this is, in a sense, something we've been 'asking for?'

Is it something that is our fate? Devolving upon us for deciding to ('daring to' to sounds too bold) live our lives this way, picking these careers, this selfish life of a poet, heedless – to the extent that we've decided to be – heedless of others?

Or, on the other hand, to what degree are we faced with the conclusion that all the lousy things that befall us are due to something else? ... That there is something inherently, unredeemably *wrong* with us? And these kinds of things are just fated to keep befalling us. And there is no escape, no remedy for it. And, perhaps, in some strange turned-on-its-head way, it is because we are, and always have been cursed in this way – and there doesn't seem to be any better term to describe this condition – *that* is why, in no small part, why we ended up becoming poets in the first place?

The follow-on question that then – it seems – needs to be posed is this: has that choice of vocation helped at all? Did it make us better, smarter? Or, did it help anyone else?

15.

Who will care about these internecine feuds?

And if no one else does, should we? Or, even if others – who come after us – do indeed care, what does it say about us that we – at this point in our lives – feel the necessity to devote so much time and energy to try, if not to settle them once and for all, then at least to get the last word in?

16.

What happens when the day comes when finally, irrevocably, we must accept our station in life?

Do we ever come to the conclusion that we've even arrived at such a place? Is it when things stop happening for us, whatever that means, or stop happening so quickly, or is it when new opportunities, possibilities, however we deign to deem them, no longer arrive on our doorstep?

Or is it when we come to believe that we've run out of gas when it comes to driving for more, for the next step? Or when it comes to our art, our careers – is it when we stop believing that there is indeed any such 'next-step,' at least for the likes of us? And then, what happens then? Is that when finally we are truly free… to do, to write, however we please – assuming of course that we haven't been writing that way all along?

Or for some of us, is that the final insult? The officer unholstering his pistol and stepping in front of the squad, all now looking down, seeing to their carbines and perhaps, depending on the occasion of the moment, collecting their spent cartridges as souvenirs.

For how many is that the most enraging of all the blows? The realization that this, this finally is it. It is *this* and nothing more? Forget about everything that one has, has done, has accomplished, put all that to the side, right now that counts for nothing. "Look at how much he or she, or those guys over there, how much they have, and why don't *I* have that… that much?" "*They* don't deserve that, they can't." It makes this entire project a joke, a lie. It's been a lie since the beginning. Hasn't it?

All of those wins, the first one, the ones that followed… How shallow, how false, how derisory. The illusions that unfolded, which led, one to another. And with each, the compromises, the lies that one is obliged to tell oneself; how they crowd upon each other. Like convicts in some bankrupt republic's overwhelmed penitentiary, built by some benign-seeming – by comparison – colonial power. The cell seemingly commodious enough at first… then more of prisoners show up, and more and more, and soon the sleeping in shifts begins.

And so it all comes to make perfect sense, doesn't it? How can it be that this should be all that there is to show for all those decades of toil, of dedication, of sacrifice? Clearly, we were robbed. There's been some malfeasance somewhere. It's not fair that we have so little and others have so much. And it is so lousy that no one listens, and no one cares.

And that last part, indubitably, is true.

17.

At what point do we say to ourselves: I need to be, I should be, I have to be happy, satisfied, resigned – perhaps, there is no way around it – with this?

And, the question, the follow-on question insists, pokes its nose under the tent: for whom does this *not* apply? Who among us, regardless of their walk of life, their instantiation in our life, in our world, in – it just may be – in any world… who amongst any of us is not obliged to ask herself or himself this very question?

For in the very same way, and is it not perhaps the same issue, the same contention, confusion or delusion… it is often said that there is always someone tougher, more deadly, or a better, more lethal fighter or combatant than *you,* than any of us, someone always out there bigger or badder, is there not? …in absolutely the same way there is always someone who has achieved, accomplished, accrued, more than any of us – at least when we look at whatever we deem as, define as accomplishment? And perhaps it is only when we reach a certain age, and have enough – enough years, enough accomplishments, enough failures, whatever, of our own – that we can draw these kinds of comparisons; comparisons between ourselves and those who we think, or used to think, we could have turned into, might in fact well have turned into had we not tried to live *this* life we've at least essayed an attempt at. So, we end up, don't we, measuring ourselves against some other – appropriately or not – some other *'we,'* in those before-dawn hours of superannuated end-stage, middle-aged fecklessness, during which we come finally to the conclusion that there is no conclusion other than we've fallen terribly short?

We lie there in the dark, through those grim, unredeeming hours, comparing ourselves to them. And they know who they are, we can be sure. And why are we not consoled by this thought: that they themselves are similarly comparing themselves to others, and finding themselves as having fallen just as decisively short?

18.

What about all those who have done better than you?

What about those who have achieved more, gotten more, raised themselves higher, garnered more of whatever it was that you all so certainly scorned when you were young – didn't you – which even now none of you, none of us, can quite cop to acknowledging means much more than nothing… For, is it not so, no matter how much any of us mayhap have managed to scoop up, there is always someone else, quite close, as it happens quite often, quite nearby as it were, who has more – and how do we come to grips with that? Especially now, after all this time?

Should we, shall we, say, tell ourselves that it has nothing, really, to do with us – our talent or our achievement – rather, instead, it is all about politics? It is all about glad-handing and brown-nosing, even in this, especially *this* world, *especially* in this poetry world? And, in fact, it is a testament to our incorruptibility, our base-level integrity, that we never bought into that – at least not completely – so, perforce, our shortfall our lack, relative or not, of renown – however denominated, compared to whomever – in fact should or must be seen as a badge of honor? And, in the final respect history, Poetry itself, will sort if all out? Won't it?

However, truth be told, might not that too be a delusion? In the same way that the young 'uns talk themselves into one fallacy or another

75

(don't they?) of ire, of revenge or irresolute shunning of us and all our works, even if they are too polite or too cowed to bring it up to us directly... decades later, might this just be another lie? Is it not possible that those who have more to show for themselves are in fact enabled to do that, to *be* that, for good and proper reasons? They've earned it, pure and simple.

19.

What do you do with all that time?

…if you've already written your masterpiece (assuming that is itself a term of art whose validity – that is to say, the morality of the terms and conditions inherent in it – is not something you find entirely absurd, much less abhorrent; in other words, it isn't a word that impels you to, say, throw up in your mouth when you hear someone else utter it)? How are you supposed to spend the rest of your natural life?

20.

How was it that we went from being careless souls to the souls of carelessness?

We, who never seemed to much care about how we lived and what we put in, or on, our bodies; now, we have trouble thinking about much else.

By now not only do we know many among us, in addition to those older than us – and often not that much older than us – who have died, it is also quite probable that we ourselves have fallen ill – at least once, quite possibly not inconsequentially, and what has been the impact of all that? How has that changed us?

Are we living our lives all that much more carefully?

21.

Is it inevitable that as we get older we grow more conservative, more cautious, more censorious, less open-minded, less, simply, flexible? Less receptive… as a matter of course, by virtue of, or according to some ineluctable, iron-clad law, some dismal code to which we are all subject?

Can we not, must we not, look at our lives, at our careers, and say: yes, this is what I was doing in my twenties and while it may surely have been more uncompromising than anything I have done since, there is a clear and compelling link or, if you will, a transition from that work to what I did in my thirties, and so, as I look back, I want to say that I see a similarly compelling and impelling force which moved me into my forties, and, again, further along, then urged me through my forties, and from my forties to my fifties… and so on. It all made, and makes sense? Or does it? This is the track, the arc, the trace of my, of one's, career – to the extent of course, that any poet can claim that she or he has a career. Right?

Nevertheless, when looking back, and unfortunately an increasing amount of looking, lately, seems, unavoidably, to be looking back, it doesn't it seem, at least for our generation, that the most radical work that we did was indeed work done in our youth… And what, assuming that is so, the question insists on being asked, what does that mean for us, as we age?

Is the carefully constructed, so artfully built-up argument that this life of writing is one of, as they say, life-long learning, is that proposition – the one that argues that the accretion of our experience, of our incrementally bulked-up skill sets – we have so much more to bring to bear, to exercise as we continue on year after year – is that all just one big lie?

22.

You of all people. You, who was never supposed to get old.

You, who was, like so many of your time, not only determined not to grow old but who definitively, defiantly, claimed to welcome an early demise instead of the decline and decay which seemed the only alternative (and how wrong were we?), an alternative which so many of our peers – we now believe we can look back and see – were all too eager to explore. You, who – we were sure, despite those foolhardy claims – would easily survive your peers, since, in fact, virtually all of them were five, ten, even more years older than you… You too, you did get old like the rest of us, or you began to.

But now you too, somehow, despite all this, despite the caveats and the conditions you called out and which we credulously – it was credulity, wasn't it – agreed to, all of that is now, like you, gone, utterly gone. And you've left us, left us here. To continue to age, while you are preserved in death, remaining not-quite-old. A remonstrance and reminder to us: this is where we too once lived, where, and when, things were just starting to go, to go downhill with some decided alacrity – what a happy time and place that seems now. And yet, that was somewhere you could not abide.

23.

Might this inclination, this predilection for the reflective, for the reflexive perhaps – for the memoir for example, be nothing more than a symptom of the loss of impetus, of momentum, of purpose, pure and simple?

Is it somehow wrong to look back, period? Should our focus somehow always remain fixed-forward, just the way it was when we were young?

There is certainly no small measure of laudable rectitude in refusing fall prey – if it is that – to the alluring entrancements of score-settling and general, across-the-board judgment. Nevertheless, perhaps it is appropriate at some point in our lives to take a look back, if for no other reason than perhaps it can, we can, thus provide others – those others who come after us – with a text and context to perhaps help them to avoid making the same mistakes we made?

Or, do we presume too much by even assuming that we will be read enough, by enough or closely enough by any who come after us, to effect any difference whatsoever?

24.

When do we agree to accept the generally-accepted 'line' or view or narrative about our times, our group, or, in the final respect, ourselves? ...However that is denominated or delineated?

Who is it, if it is anyone, who decides that this is *'the'* definition for us? Even if – or, particularly so – especially if that definition is *no* definition at all? If, in fact, our fate is not to be mis-defined, poorly appreciated or unfairly assessed or maligned, in fact – but, to the contrary, to be subject to something else entirely? If 'subject' is in fact at all the proper term at all. So, what we are talking about is *not* a relative lack of attention but, instead, a totalizing supernal disregard. 'We are going to ignore you in entire, jointly and severally, every jot and tittle, down to your smallest instance and iteration?' Then what?

25.

Those who can't accept their fate with dignity – do we, should we, think any less of them?

We may not bear it well. And, what if, when it comes to people like us, if we just fall apart as the blows begin to fall?

What do you expect from us anyway? We did our bit. We did our part (and what, pray tell, have you done?) did we not? If now, in the face of all that we now by virtue of such skill and mettle or just plain thoughtless, disinterested luck, that has seen us survive so far, we have to end up dealing with all of this – this aging, this obsolescence, this disease, this decrepitude – why shouldn't we react in just the self-same way as so many of us do?

Isn't it a perfectly natural response? Who can blame us? If only… if only it were not for those, those others, the ones who don't cry out in the night. The ones who do not complain. The ones who don't slip, don't slow down. The ones who, while certainly looking over their shoulder, don't slacken their pace even one step as the weather increases, in the face of just the kind of storm which we – we would, we did, we will, indeed, we will certainly – succumb to, but through which they, unlike us, it seems, somehow persevere.

26.

And if, or, rather, when the body begins to fail, does that mean the mind is not far behind?

But are we now, somehow free in a way we never could be before? Or is this too another vain wish? Might it be that we remain and will forever be, for as long as we are alive, witting, able and vexed women and men? Or is that a vain thought? But, if so, in some way are we then obliged to continue to be tied into, bound into, bound up with this strange vitality, this irreducible force that perhaps we, in all probability should admit is not just a decent self-regard but in fact, a version of *vanity* itself, and nothing less? And is it this, this vanity which we tender as a demonstration, as evidence self-evident of our continued attendance, our vitality, so proffered?

We are still here. We're still alive. At least that's our argument.

27.

Is there anything that can armor us or at least, in some way, serve us well, or, at least, not turn on us – in the way that so many of things that we pinned our hopes on ended up disappointing us, to put it mildly – as we hove forward into this future for which we feel so utterly unprepared?

Laughter. *There does seem to be one quality, one dimension when it comes to the ways we contracted with each other, at least some of us did, and similarly engaged with the world, which, at the time, seemed like a luxury or perhaps an acquired taste or, possibly, a quality – let's call it that – which one might or might not possess in a notable way or not, but which now seems utterly necessary. It appears now as a requirement, an obvious requisite, an iron-framed absolute without which it well neigh seems inconceivable to frankly carry on without: we must maintain a sense of humor.*

If we cannot laugh, at each other, at all of those who have come after us (those who came before us have doubtless weathered enough already of our scorn and jibe), *at you,* and, especially if we cannot laugh at ourselves, at us, and at the fix we've found ourselves in, at the pretty pass we've pitched up at, this lovely forenoon, then really and truly, we are in trouble. Well, we know we're in trouble already, but sans that saving grace we are really and truly sunk… And, more to the point, those among us – those of our rank (such as it is) and seniority (to frame it, albeit, with air quotes around that term) who don't, or can't summon up, or feel it beneath them, or – indeed – are suffering so, so much that they can't find it within themselves (and we dare not disrespect that particular condition) to laugh at themselves, they are, it is to be feared, doubtlessly lost.

Or, if they are not already sunk in perdition, surely they are at terrible risk.

We must keep laughing, if for no other reason than to save ourselves, at least for the time being.

28.

Is there anything *we should feel entitled to feel good about?*

Perhaps the fact that we're still here? We may be lame or halt or irrelevant or – irrelevant *and* ridiculous, but the fact remains that we're still here. We still show up. Or, we should.

And while there may be some – who are not all that much younger than us – who surely wish we'd give up and, once and for all, stop stepping on their scene; that is, stop sucking the air out of the room in our insufferable boomer-ist way; nevertheless, the very fact that we can still make an appearance, that must count for something. One would think.

For a few years there was a certain novelty factor which exercised a degree of sway over us: the time had come – as it comes to us all, should we be so lucky – that whenever we showed up at a reading or an event, a conference, a book party, we were always the oldest there. It was odd, it was at first disconcerting; surely there must be some mistake. Someone must be out of town, or ill, or, eventually it came suggest itself, had – with a certain crashing rudeness – decided to go ahead and drop dead sans any sense of decent fair warning.

At first it just did not make sense that we should be the oldest there. Now, it is the custom and the practice. You look around the room, scanning the faces – and the heads, before the lights dim; and the heads themselves, even more than the faces – tell you all you need to know.

How few are there here with gray hair? How many fewer whose hair, if there's any left, has gone white? Now, no one expects to see anyone at a reading who is our own age, much less anyone older. And if one of one's friends should appear, what a holiday is that? Make way! Clear some seats! There's more than one of us in the house; more than one of us still getting it together to get around.

As young poets, filing meekly into our seats at St. Marks, for how many years, year upon year, did we catch sight of Edwin Denby, that intimate of the immortals, frail and snowy brow'd, a beautiful and wondrously generous man who'd been friends with, stood by, supported and advocated for so many of the greats? There he'd be, sitting by himself, impossibly old.

The sprinkle of white hair. Looking on, quietly off to the side; showing up for the younger poets. How much older was he then than we are now? Not much. Not so much. Not much older than us. Perhaps not older than us at all.

So... we still show up, at least now and then. And if we deem it right and proper that we should commandeer the first row, who is there who would begrudge us that? I mean, we could be home, warm and comfortable – or, at least, warm – but instead we're out and about. And maybe that should count something.

And for the benefit of all those who are ten, twenty, thirty, forty years younger than us... Might it be that by merely showing up we are performing some sort of social good? Or, on the other hand, might we not be just annoying further those whose most pressing wish is that we should simply shuffle off the stage as soon as possible, having hogged the limelight for so many more years than ever we have should? Nonetheless, are we not demonstrating that it is possible to have a life, to 'conduct' a life, to come out through the other end, whole? …that it is not necessary to burn up in the upper atmosphere? …that you can indeed make a safe landing or, if not, at least parachute to earth, and live to tell the tale?

Show up, and listen and pay attention too… You might learn something. Might that be the most important lesson, or the last lesson, we have to impart to those who come after us? Greater than, perhaps, any of the arguments we tried to posit in our poems, or tried to point to by the way we wrote our poems or wrote about our poems, or each other's poems?

A Spectre is Haunting
the Poetry World

1.

Get me Kevin McCarthy! I don't care if he's dead! Who's his agent?

God, where's Kevin McCarthy (or Donald Sutherland, if we're talking remake) when you need him? But instead of running through those 1950s California small town streets screaming, "They're here! They're here!" We need someone to stand up and shout: "It's here. It's here too!" The diagnosis – he played a doctor, remember? – is so very similar. Instead of 'Invasion of the Body Snatchers,' what we have here is 'The Invasion of Trickle-Down Economics.'

The yawning, increasing injustice, the accelerating inequality in our society, in every industrialized country, is perfectly mirrored by the gaping, growing inequality we see in our own world, in the poetry world. It's here too.

A rentier class sits at the top, lolling, gamboling, drinking deeply of all that's good and rarefied up there. There they are, the grandees, the hedge fund managers, the academic administrators too, astride it all, peering down from the commanding heights: the same 1%, the one tenth of 1%, the one hundredth of 1%. Well, actually, they're all not pulling up to the Casino in Monte Carlo in yellow Lambos, some of them are getting by, much more humbly, with Volvos in Westhampton. Although, others might say, that sure beats the hell out of the A train to the Rockaways.

And we see everywhere else the same struggling: the constant scrimping and insecurity, in what's supposed to be the safe 'middle,' and the desperate scrabbling attempts to make a living, to scrape out a life, towards the bottom.

Some, however, see through this. They see the few at the top who have prospered spectacularly at the expense of everyone else. They see through the fatuous lies soberly pronounced about why this is so, why it has to be so, the debased ideology that everyone is supposed to buy into… Here too, even here.

There is a specter haunting the poetry world.

2.

Would you like fries with that MFA?

And just what are you whining about now? You're living in your car – so what? – and commuting four hours a day from one adjunct community college gig to another while trying to make ends meet waiting tables at Red Lobster, hoping against hope they don't ask you to *clopen* again, for the fourth day in a row, all the while trying to figure out whether you make just a bit too much or just a bit too little to qualify for coverage on that health exchange, what do you have to complain about? You're living the dream!

And, has there ever come a time when you're waiting on a table, it's a four-top but there are only three people there, and you realize sitting there, looking up at you, twisting the paper napkin in her hands, what do you know, here's one of your students. You are waiting on her. And not just her. But her parents too.

"Mom, Dad, this is my creative writing instructor…"

Those looks on Mom's and Dad's face, aren't they just delicious? As they glance up from the laminated menu with the Catch of the Day, laser-printed and slotted into that special leatherette holder, their eyes passing from her face to yours and back again, as they say to themselves, "This, *this* is what my child has to look forward to? This is why I'm spending all that money of ours, so she can end up like this?"

"Hi, my name is Dawn and I'll be your daughter's guide to literary self-realization this semester. And now I'd like to tell you about tonight's Endless Shrimp specials."

3.

C'mon, why don't you tell us how you really feel?

Zebra mussels aren't so bad. And, those wooly adelgids, did one of them ever bother you? It's not like they arrived at our shores in the ballast of some rusty Liberian-flagged freighter; or in the checked luggage of some well-meaning zoologist possessed of the half-cocked notion that this new species would rid us of some apparently intractable native pest but instead ran rampant – like some once-cute marsupial we originally thought of as exotic but which now we hire guys who wear Tyvek suits and booties to rid our drainage canals or septic fields of. It's not like that at all.

There's not the slightest similarity to kudzu. But at some point the question needs to be asked: this metastasis of creative writing programs far and wide... It's not a localized recurrence any more, we're way past that. What, or who, got that going in the first place?

But if there weren't as many programs as there are, there wouldn't be as many jobs as in fact there are. And how lucky is it that there are so many of us who, in a way that was unthinkable not that many decades ago, are bid free to live this particular life: that is to say... we can make a living, have a life, maybe even a family, take a vacation now and then, have health coverage and dental too and maybe something getting put away for retirement... and have all this and to be paid and to spend every day at work working at something we care for more than anything. To be able to talk about poetry and the writing of it, and get paid for it, to spend one's 9 to 5 doing that, how lucky is that?

But what about the kids who need to fill the seats? Some say that poetry isn't production work, but they're wrong. Everyone, the tenured as much as the adjuncts, in a way, are all working to quota, no? We have to have enough bodies to fill the seats. And this is the world we live in. This is what work means nowadays in this world. If there are no students then we don't need the program and if we don't need the program we don't need that position, and then we don't need to pay you. We don't need you.

And as for their years in this better place, those kids, how should we think about them? Some have called these few years, however many they turn out to be: two, four, more, as a singularly special, almost sanctified time… it will be the last time they will be able to get up in the morning and do what they should be able to do day in and day out for all their days: write, read, think about poetry. That's what they were set upon this world to do and should be able to do, and should be able to spend their lives doing, if there was any justice in this world, of which, as is so patently, clearly, blindingly, obvious that it must needs be repeated, and repeated often… there is virtually none, or none.

And then we look back at this world we do spend ourselves in, every work day. And we hope this isn't simply a place into which so many of those young souls are inveigled and then swiftly weighted down, so many of them, with crushing debt, and not much more. We can only hope that this is more than simply a place where eventually they are garlanded with degrees they cannot possibly turn to advantage or leverage for any purpose, save perhaps for enmeshing them, in turn, because what other options might there be, into a coruscating, immersating life of contingent-academic labor as indentured, itinerant tinkers slaving away in far-flung satrapies, shaping-up each dawn for day-work in these dark academic mills.

4.

Wait! Where did everyone go? They were here just a minute ago.

What would Darwin say? Is it a matter of survival of the artistically fittest?

Maybe it's the same kind of question some people are asking these days over on the Upper East Side... Why is it that no doctors or lawyers have apartments on Park Avenue anymore? Have they... even they... been priced out? Why does it seem like absolutely every building along that stretch, from the Sixties to the Eighties, is stuffed with hedge fund managers and private equity guys, from the storage rooms and private wine cellars to what used to be the servants' rooms in the attics?

What does it say about how bad things have gotten, how out of hand things are, when your modest, unprepossessing, run-of-the-mill Fortune 500 CEO can no longer afford a prewar Fifth Avenue Rosario Candela Classic 9 with a white-glove-attended elevator opening on its own entrance gallery? What's he to do? Where's he to turn? Where do we expect him to go? Sutton Place? Central Park West? Really? Is this what we've come to?

Is it possible that in the same way that the powers-that-be have completed the financialization of our economy, we've similarly, largely, remade, that is to say deformed, with the equivalent of hedge fund managers and private equity guys, big swathes of the poetry world to similarly reflect ourselves and our newfound values? Is this the world we all live in now? Everyone's in finance now, right?

Is that why there's so much getting published nowadays that all sounds alike. In fact, some might say that it all sounds like just like one or two of us, and what those one or two of us were doing thirty or forty years ago?

Back in the early days of Language poetry, of Flarf, of Conceptualism, of any upheaval, of, for example, Cubism or Surrealism or Abstract Expressionism or Pop or Minimalism, or Bebop or folk music or rock and roll, or was there more variety, more diversity? And if so, how and why did that variegation dry up, fall away? And now when we think of that kind of work why do we think of the kind of work that is exemplified by just a handful of its original practitioners?

Is that sort of monoculture an inescapable evolution of the maturity of any particular style, as the full flowering of any new kind of writing/thinking/creating simply ages, as it gets older? But what about those alternate iterations? Were they in any way inferior? Is that why they are no longer with us? No longer getting any attention?

5.

Thrilling, terrifying, explosive

But, the thing is, so many people are already free. So many people are already doing wild, scary, breathtaking work, work that we could never imagine doing ourselves. And they are all around us. They are not afraid.

They are not afraid of the scorn. They are not afraid to be told that someone thirty or forty years older than they did the same thing back in the 1970s – which is a lie. They are not afraid, so many of them, perhaps most of them, that they won't get tenure because they've already figured out that that isn't in the cards. They know who they are.

How they are making a go of it, how they are making a living, is another story.

Perhaps they have accepted that there isn't, won't be, can't be, any nexus, any relationship between what they do, day in and day out, to put a roof over their head and what they were put on this earth to do, how they are supposed to – indeed – live out their days. They are living the life they are supposed to be living. They are here to point out to us what's real and what's not. They're doing their job. We need to recognize them and what they're doing, their work, their good works, the best we can. That's our job.

6.

What would a dictatorship of the Precariat look like?

We go to the appointed place. It's a poetry reading. We sit. Someone gets up to read. She or he starts in… and suddenly we are taken to a place we've never been before. A place we could never have imagined. A wild, free, frightening, hilarious, breathtaking place.

They tilt back their heads and the words flow out. The voices are strong and unafraid. That all-too common, deathly, churchy, flattened poetry-reading-voice – pitched high and voiced in the back of the mouth so as not to offend but to make it clear that this isn't everyday speech – no, none of that. Not here, not now. This is real poetry. All that narcissistic, passive-aggressive, false modesty has no place here today. These voices are clear and free.

Isn't this what poetry is supposed to do? Take us there, somewhere, and bring us back? Put us back down in our seats, not let us catch our breath. And then, finally, release us out to the streets where we look about ourselves: the world is the same; the city looks the same… but it isn't.

The cheap pizzeria on West Third Street with its glaring yellow and red signage and the fake-Irish tavern with its sham paneling, they are as garish as ever. The drunk NYU students are just as loud, the sidewalk as soiled and sticky, the westbound Saturday night traffic streaming cross-town, just as unforgiving. The crowds surge up from the West 4th Street station. They've come to town from Brooklyn, from

Queens, from the Bronx. They swarm along Sixth, past the playground and the famous basketball court on the east side of the street, past the movie theater on the west. As endless as they ever were, as full of pulsing, throbbing, buzzing life as were their great-grand parents when Reginald Marsh painted them a hundred years ago, when Weegee and Abbott and Frank and Winogrand snapped them so many years ago, when everyone from Hopper to de Kooning to Andy, from Millay to Cummings to Allen to O'Hara, and Robert Zimmerman too as he turned himself into Dylan, and all the rest, walked these same streets. But something is different. We'll never be able to see any of this quite the same way again – that's what those poems we heard today did to us, did for us.

And cutting through the slow-moving, northbound river of cabs and cars and vans, we very well may see a long red fire truck shoulder past, its siren tolling, pushing up the avenue. If it's a hook-and-ladder, it will be from that 70s brick firehouse, the one that sits, just a little way downtown, at the intersection of Houston and Sixth and Bedford, its entrance decked with 9/11 plaques saluting officers and men who never returned that day.

And on the front of that truck will be a shining '5.' It is the same number "5 in gold" that William Carlos Williams caught sight of just a few blocks from here one day almost a hundred years ago, which he immortalized in The Great Figure, that work of genius, and which his friend Charles Demuth then memorialized in his masterpiece which now hangs in the Metropolitan. It is the same storied fire company, and it is that same glorious fire truck's direct, lineal descendent, rolling over these very same streets. The same streets these young poets now pace, taking everything in, transmuting all this, just as Williams did, into their own gold.

They get it, these poets. They understand what it means to be members of the Precariat. They understand their power.

They are doing the hard work. They know who they are. They have nothing to lose. The world, this world, is going to belong to them.

Thanks to the following writers who read the preceding three essays in earlier versions or discussed with me the questions the essays seek to address, and were generous enough with their time to share their insight. This work is the better for their comments:

Charles Alexander, Bruce Andrews, Steve Benson, Brandon Brown, Miles Champion, Vlad Davidzon, Alan Davies, Katie Degentesh, Rob Fitterman, Drew Gardner, Nada Gordon, Isabel Gottlieb, Brenda Iijima, Allan Jalon, Nathan Kernan, Jack Kimball, Wayne Koestenbaum, Andrew Levy, Sharon Mesmer, Bob Perelman, Trace Peterson, Nick Piombino, Kit Robinson, Michael Scharf, James Sherry, Rodrigo Toscano, John Tranter, Geoff Young, Mark Young, Scott Zieher, Steve Zultanski

Author's Afterword

This, I didn't want to have to write.

Kenny is wrong. And everything he has done here has been wrong. That goes for Vanessa too.

First some background: about a year ago a firestorm erupted in what we call the poetry world, as many of the readers of this likely already know. The proximate cause of this firestorm was a performance that Kenneth Goldsmith gave at Brown University, during which he read a version of the autopsy report of Michael Brown, the black youth killed by a white policeman in Ferguson, Missouri. The work of another prominent Conceptualist poet, Vanessa Place, who had been posting portions of 'Gone With The Wind,' line-by-line on Twitter, also became part of this controversy and debate. While this was happening I was finishing up the third of the essays in this book.

I didn't want to write this but I don't see how I can remain silent. I didn't want to write this in no small part because I believe strongly in this kind of writing, the kind of writing that's under attack now – for it is not just those two poets who are under attack, Conceptualism itself has been attacked and condemned. I need to say that I believe that Conceptualism, along with another movement that has gained prominence in this part of the poetry world, known as Flarf, represent the two most important, most interesting, most intriguing and exciting developments in poetry in years. I believed that before this storm brewed up, I believe it still.

I also didn't want to write this, frankly, because Kenny Goldsmith has been very good to me. I've known him a long time. A few years ago, Kenny co-edited a definitive and voluminous Conceptualist anthology. As many readers of this surely know, it is always an important inflection point in the life of a literary movement when its first anthology comes to be published. I was asked to contribute some work to that anthology, along with just a few other poets from previous generations. It was flattering and gratifying to be included.

Also, I have to admit, among my first reactions as this storm brewed up was this: all of those who were criticizing Kenny and Vanessa were just more academics, I told myself, albeit ones on the younger side, and this was just another inside-baseball story. That is, this was a fight over academic perquisites and power, over who gets to pick the speaking slots at conferences, for example, and really nothing more. And, the fact is, much of this book seeks to raise basic questions about just those conferences, just that academicization of the poetry world, and what – in my opinion, and many others, that development, that academicization, has done to poetry, to the poetry world, to poets. So, as the debate over Kenny and Vanessa continued, I grew troubled that the argument I am here, in this book, trying to put forward, particularly in the third essay of this book – regarding the malign effects, especially notable since the recent economic crisis, engendered by the transformation of the poetry world, which my generation of poets did so much to make happen – would be diluted or muddied, or the argument it tried to make, the questions it asked, would be eclipsed, would be put into the shade, by this firestorm.

I also didn't want to write this out of a concern that whatever I say here comes across like the complaints or rants of another out-of-touch old white poet. But then I came to realize that if a reader of A Spectre is Haunting the Poetry World, the third essay in this book… say, for example someone whose life is not all that different than one of hypothetical poets portrayed in that essay, like that young poet, working as a adjunct, pulling down a shift at Red Lobster to pay the bills, who is obliged to use her car as her office, if she's not in fact living in her car, who finds herself waiting on one of her students and her parents… if she read this, it occurred to me, and saw that there's no reference at all to what is going on now in the poetry world – this storm around Kenny and Vanessa – that might very seem wrong, if not downright suspicious, to her.

The thing is, as I have read the postings, the long and thoughtful responses to Kenny's and Vanessa's work, as I have listened, I have come to realize that, in fact, I was wrong. This is not an inside-baseball story among and between academics positioning for power. Nor is it about free speech. Then again, it is. I won't presume to speak for others here, others who have eloquently, far more eloquently than I can, laid out everything that is wrong about what Kenny and Vanessa have done, nor everything that is wrong when it comes to what has been said on their behalf – including especially that profile in the New Yorker. Nor can or should I presume here to recapitulate the full range of the arguments that have been arrayed. Nor, in the final respect do I believe this can be deemed an example of calling-out, that internet-enabled naming and shaming phenomenon.

But it is clear now, even to me, that 'free speech' is an argument that has been, and continues often, to be used by the powerful to silence others. It is wheeled into place, its trucks groaning, its rifled barrel swabbed and readied, like an aged but still serviceable, still dangerous, piece of field artillery. All arguments that involve speech are not always, or only, about freedom-of-speech. We know that the white musicians in 19th century America who donned black face defended their so-called minstrelsy using freedom-of-speech arguments while they grew rich and famous. And they were not just stealing others' speech, and art, while simultaneously maligning and defaming others. As they were doing so they were silencing them, those black artists who had originally created that speech, that art. They were able to pull off that trick – those white artists – in no small part by situating themselves so that they were empowered to put forth the claim that they in fact 'owned' that speech. And they used freedom-of-speech arguments to do so.

And certainly there are examples aside from minstrelsy that we can look at, examples that aren't found in the relatively distant past; examples where the dirty work of power is garbed in the spotless raiment of free speech and thus deemed untouchable. We can't criticize it: money is transformed into free speech. For example, that Supreme

Court case we call 'Citizens United.' How different is that?

So, Kenny and Vanessa weren't just appropriating, or borrowing. Because of the places and roles they hold, or held, in this world, this part of the poetry world, I have come to agree with those who say that they were objectively seeking to colonialize, to own, and exclude others from the actual space wherein that speech could take place. And who were those arguing so? They were just those younger writers, mostly of color, some anonymous, others not, whom I had initially deemed as nothing more than practitioners of poetry world inside-baseball, including the anonymous Mongrel Coalition Against Gringpo. Paying attention to them has helped me understand this. Others engaged in important work on this whom I have learned from include Kathy Park Hong, Fred Moten, Jen Hofer, Juliana Spahr and Stephanie Young.

And then a few months later, a few months after this all blew up, during which nothing at all was heard from Kenny, a profile in the New Yorker appeared. And how did that profile of Kenny Goldsmith come across? The free speech argument is trotted out again. This time it is garbed in the robes of the embattled avant garde artist who is suffering, who is being punished for being provocative, for pushing boundaries, for being brave, for that is how Kenny is depicted, and quoted. Quotes from various and sundry supporters are sprinkled into a mise-en-scene: Kenny hanging out in his Chelsea loft. Someone, a famous critic – the self-appointed academic kingmaker for the Language Poets and the Conceptualists too – just happens to phone in while the reporter just happens to be sitting there (a New Yorker staffer of long and prominent tenure; a guy who I was friends with in college). How serendipitous. The famous academic tells Kenny to hang tough.

And what, pray tell, might that adjunct getting off her shift at Red Lobster say to herself when she read that piece? I can't presume to speak for her but I wouldn't be surprised if it came across like the establishment, the power structure, the white power structure, had decided to protect one of their own. The New Yorker is putting down the hammer: 'don't you mess with one of ours.'

This is not going away. It is clear that this storm is not going to blow over quickly, as some would wish. This is not a tempest in a teapot. The fault lines that have been exposed here, the contradictions and the lies and the bullying that was par for the course for so many years, as they all become unearthed, lying there before us, as they continue to be examined, picked apart, analyzed, as they must, all this ensures that this storm will continue to blow, as it should, as it must.

As the storm continues, more poets are weighing in and providing additional insights regarding this world, this poetry; what this world is truly made of, made up of, how it is organized. And as we read those analyses, some of us we may for the first time be coming to realize just how much privilege, privilege so variously denominated, has informed, for our entire life, in so many ways, how indeed we look at the world.

Nevertheless, I continue to believe in these kinds of writing, these forms. This kind of writing is so powerful. It is central, it is key, it is and has been among the most powerful, vital and transformative writing we've seen in our time. But the fact is Conceptualism, like Flarf, and like, it must be admitted, Language writing itself, I am starting to see, have had an impact in our world, in our history, that has not necessarily in all times and all places been in fact 'neutral.' For example, I am starting to understand how over the years these kinds of writing were often used, in essence, to silence others. And here I am not referring to the doomed, old-style kinds of poetry we set our caps against when we were young, the tired, worn-out styles of poetry we disdained and whose practitioners we deemed our hereditary foes, whose writing we indeed wanted to do down. We saw that as our job. I'm not talking about them or that kind of writing,

On the contrary, we need to think long and hard about the impact that our types of avant garde poetry, like Language writing and like Conceptualism, have had in other ways. There are analyses being published now that tell us when it comes to creative writing programs, the more elite they are, and the more they focus on the kind of writing I believe in, it turns out that – the whiter they are. I believe we need to think about how those kinds of writing have played a role in enforcing a conformity in those programs, along what pass for the corridors of power in the poetry world, and to what degree that conformity was white. And that sober re-consideration needs also be undertaken by those among us who never trod those corridors, who were never comfortable that those corridors ever became accessible to the likes of us, back several decades ago.

Could it be, perhaps, that one cannot, on one's own, develop sufficient consciousness to, for example, correctly apperceive how much privilege – privilege that we may not have ever been aware of, but were born with – informs one's own viewpoints? Is that not why it is important keep a hand in when it comes to that skill, the one which poets are supposed to be really good at: seeing, and listening?

Listening is not everything that we need to be good at in order to be a poet but we can say that poets do need to listen good and hard. And then they need take what they have heard and seen, whatever is sensational or inconceivable and then try and make sense of it, even or especially if that 'sense' is a sense that the rest of us have never contemplated before. Making sense of it may mean just figuring out how to put it all into words. Turning it all into words, the actual writing, is the last part. That's the writing. And before the writing comes the sense-making, and before that comes the listening, or the seeing. That is what comes first.

This is not a definition that fits everyone and everything that gets created when it comes to poetry. It would be unfair and just plain wrong to claim that it defines the conditions and stages or steps when it comes to how all poetry or art is created. Nevertheless, if I am starting to understand the things written about in this essay, and I think I am just starting to understand them, it is because – and I hope I am not patting myself on the back – I am still at least somewhat capable of taking first step when it comes to doing what we do as poets, that is: listening.

I know I don't hear as well as I used to. I have to get my hearing tested regularly now. There's the tinnitus, which seems to be getting worse. And maybe I don't see as well as I used to, either. Every time I go to the eye doctor, the prescription I get handed is stronger than the last. But I want to believe I can still make out some things.

Of course, it is clear that eventually much more than listening is going to have to happen in order to change things. But for all of us, I'd argue, listening is the beginning. For some of us, maybe, listening is all that we will be capable of. Doing more than mere listening may be the job of others, others who are younger.

Acknowledgements

Jobs of the Poets first appeared in *Jacket* magazine and then in my book *Memoir And Essay*, published by Faux Books and Other Publications.

Letters to a Middle Aged Poet originally appeared in the magazine *Otoliths*.

Thanks to the editors and publishers of those books and journals.

About the Author

Michael Gottlieb is the author of nineteen books including most recently, *I Had Every Intention, Dear All,* and *Memoir And Essay,* the authoritative recounting of the early days of the Language school. He was one of the editors of *Roof,* the foundational 1970s and 80s poetry magazine. A number of his works have been adopted for the stage, including his definitive 9/11 poem, *The Dust,* hailed by Ron Silliman as one of the "five greatest Language poems." *The Dust* was staged by Fiona Templeton and company at the Poetry Project at St. Marks on the tenth anniversary of 9/11.

About Chax

Founded in 1984 in Tucson, Arizona, the mission of Chax is to create community through the publication of books of poetry and related literature that are works of excellence and vision, and through the presentation of poets and other artists in public programs as well as in dialogue with each other in symposia. Chax has published nearly 200 books in a variety of formats, including hand printed letterpress books and chapbooks, hybrid digital and letterpress chapbooks, book arts editions, and trade paperback editions such as the book you are holding. In August 2014 Chax moved to Victoria, Texas, and is presently located in the University of Houston Victoria Center for the Arts.

Recent and current books-in-progress include *Lizard*, by Sarah Rosenthal, *Dark Ladies*, by Steve McCaffery, *Andalusia*, by Susan Thackrey, *Limerence & Lux*, by Saba Razvi, *Short Course*, by Ted Greenwald & Charles Bernstein, *Diesel Hand*, by Nico Vassilakis, *An Intermittent Music*, by Ted Pearson, *The Collected Poems of Gil Ott*, and several other books to come.

You may find CHAX online at *http://chax.org*

Usborne Naturetrail
Rocks &
Fossils

These are crystals of a
mineral called quartz, which
is found in many rocks.

Usborne Naturetrail

Rocks & Fossils

Struan Reid

Designed by
Michael Hill and Kate Rimmer

Illustrated by
Brin Edwards, Non Figg
and Ian Jackson

Edited by Jane Chisholm and Susanna Davidson

Consultant: Professor Dorrik Stow,
University of Southampton National Oceanography Centre

Usborne Quicklinks

The Usborne Quicklinks website is packed with thousands of links to all the best websites on the internet. The websites include information, video clips, sounds, games and animations that support and enhance the information in Usborne Internet-linked books.

To visit the recommended websites for Naturetrail Rocks & Fossils, go to the Usborne Quicklinks Website at **www.usborne.com/quicklinks** and enter the keywords: **naturetrail rocks**.

When using the internet please follow the internet safety guidelines displayed on the Usborne Quicklinks website.

The recommended websites in Usborne Quicklinks are regularly reviewed and updated, but Usborne Publishing Ltd. is not responsible for the content or availability of any website other than its own. We recommend that children are supervised while using the internet.

This fish died as it was eating another fish, and then both were fossilized.

CONTENTS

Rock spotting

8 Rocks, rocks everywhere
10 Rocks or minerals?
12 Looking for rocks
14 A walk in the country
16 Beachcombing
18 Towns and gardens

The restless Earth

22 A warm heart
24 Our moving world
26 Weather and weathering

Rocks

30 Hot rocks
32 Igneous rocks to spot
34 Layered rocks
36 Sedimentary rocks to spot
38 Making new rocks
40 Metamorphic rocks to spot
42 Using rocks

Minerals

46 Mineral building blocks
48 Crystal patterns
50 Making minerals
52 Rock-forming minerals
54 Gemstones
56 Precious gemstones to spot
58 Semi-precious gemstones
60 Minerals and metals
62 Ore minerals to spot

Fossils

66 What are fossils?
68 Classifying fossils
70 Looking for fossils
72 Fossil fuels
74 What fossils can tell us
76 The past and the future
78 Fossils from the sea to spot
80 Plant and animal fossils

Rock collecting

84 Starting a collection
86 Preparing your collection
88 Collecting fossils
90 Glossary
94 Index
96 Acknowledgements

These granite and quartz pebbles have been tumbled and washed into shape by the sea.

Rock spotting

Everywhere you go, you're surrounded by rocks, even if you haven't noticed it. Our homes are made of materials that come from rocks. The moment you step outside the door, you'll be walking on ground that's covered in paving stones or rocks of one kind or another.

An incredible amount of information is stored away inside them – and it can tell us a lot about the amazing history of our planet.

Keep your eyes open – because it won't be long before you bump up against a rock of some sort.

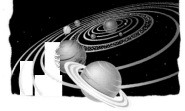

PRIME POSITION

Planet Earth is part of a family of planets, known as the Solar System, which revolve around a star we call the Sun.

Earth is the third planet from the Sun. This means that it receives just the right amount of heat and light to support living things.

Rocks, rocks everywhere

Our Earth is made up of rocks and minerals. You can see them all around you – on mountain tops and in cliff faces, in deep valleys, riverbeds and on beaches. Even the homes we live in are made from stone and building materials, such as bricks, cement and glass, which are all created from rocks and minerals.

A delicate shell

Our planet is divided up into three main parts: a thin, shell-like surface called the crust, then a layer of solid and hot liquid rock called the mantle, and a boiling hot bit in the middle called the core.

The closer to the core of the Earth, the hotter it gets. These boiling hot layers sometimes burst out as volcanoes, shooting molten (melted) rock, ash and gases into the air.

The mantle is made up of white-hot rock, about 2,900km (1,800 miles) thick.

Outer core

Inner core

The core consists of an outer part of molten metal, and a solid metal inner core.

The Earth's surface or crust is a thin, rocky shell, just 5-70km (3-43 miles) thick.

A mine of information

Studying the rocks and minerals that make up the Earth is called geology, and the people who study them are called geologists.

Rocks contain an extraordinary amount of information about the story of the Earth and how it was formed thousands of millions of years ago. With each discovery about how and when the rocks were formed, geologists can tell us more of the incredible story of what's going on beneath our feet.

This striking rock formation is Black Church Rock in southern England. It was laid down in horizontal layers, but over millions of years these have been pushed up vertically.

DISTANT MESSAGES

Geologists sometimes gather information about rocks on other planets by studying meteorites – rocky fragments that have landed on Earth from space.

Some meteorites show that some of the rocks on other planets are very similar to those found on Earth.

If you look closely at this piece of granite, you can see that it's made of a mixture of different minerals.

Magnified view of granite

Quartz

Dark mica

Pink feldspar

Rocks or minerals?

Minerals are the building blocks that rocks are made of. They consist of simple chemical substances called elements. Some minerals, such as gold and diamond, contain just a single element, but most minerals are combinations of two or more elements.

Rocks are solid mixtures of minerals – two, three or more of them. If you look very closely at a rock, you can sometimes see the different minerals inside it.

Geologists divide rocks into three main types, according to the way they were formed. (You can find out more about this on pages 30-41.)

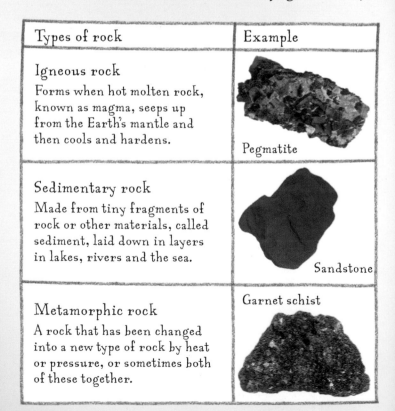

Types of rock	Example
Igneous rock Forms when hot molten rock, known as magma, seeps up from the Earth's mantle and then cools and hardens.	Pegmatite
Sedimentary rock Made from tiny fragments of rock or other materials, called sediment, laid down in layers in lakes, rivers and the sea.	Sandstone
Metamorphic rock A rock that has been changed into a new type of rock by heat or pressure, or sometimes both of these together.	Garnet schist

Soft and wet

You might think of rocks
as being hard, but in fact
they come in different forms.
Soft clay and sand are rocks
too. Some rocks are even created
by the slow dripping of water over
millions of years. These form hanging
spikes known as stalactites, or dripstones.

Stalactites like these
grow about 2cm (1in)
every 120 years.

What are fossils?

Fossils are the preserved remains of animals
and plants that lived thousands or millions
of years ago. A fossil forms when a dead
plant or animal is buried under sediment,
which turns to sedimentary rock. The
remains decay, and the space is
usually filled with
minerals.

Sometimes hard
parts such as shells
survive – as you
can see in this
fossil of a turtle.

HOW FOSSILS ARE MADE

Fossils are created
when sediment, such
as sand or mud, is
washed or blown over
the remains of plants
or animals. As they
rot away, the space
fills with minerals
from the sediment
and from water.

Fossilization takes
place by pure chance,
only if the remains
are buried quickly.

Looking for rocks

You don't need a lot of equipment on a rock-spotting trip, but a few simple things will be very useful to carry with you.

Map in hand

One of the most important things to take is a good map of the area, so you know where to look. It should show the shape of the land and the main rock outcrops to be seen, as well as any towns, roads and paths.

Here is a very simple illustration of some of the features you should find on your map.

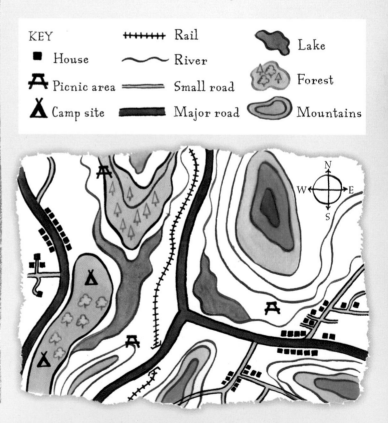

KEY
- ■ House
- ♠ Picnic area
- ⛺ Camp site
- ┼┼┼┼┼ Rail
- ∿ River
- ═══ Small road
- ▬▬ Major road
- Lake
- Forest
- Mountains

WHAT TO TAKE

Here's a list of some of the main things to take with you on your trip to find rocks and fossils.

* A detailed map of the area, or a street map if you're exploring a town.

* A notebook and pen to record your discoveries and make sketches.

* A magnifying lens for close-up inspections of interesting rocks.

* A small hammer and trowel to dig out rocks. A geologist's hammer is best, if you can get one.

* A zip-lock bag to carry any specimens you find. Newspaper is good for packing fragile stones.

* A field guide with clear illustrations to help you identify your rock finds.

* You can find out more information about starting a rock and fossil collection on pages 84-89.

Choosing a field guide

Before choosing a guide, make sure it covers the range of rocks you are likely to see in your area. It should be divided into sections on minerals, rocks and fossils. For example, can you find these fossils in the guide below?

Compare these fossils to the ones in your guide. Do they have the same patterns on them?

Echinoid fossils

1. Flip through the guide. Is your example easy to find?

2. What are the illustrations like? Is it easy to recognize your rock or fossil example?

3. Are the words clear and easy to read?

4. Does the description tell you all you want to know?

INSIDE YOUR GUIDE

*Your guide should show the rocks divided into three groups: igneous, sedimentary and metamorphic.

*Minerals should be divided into three main groups: rock-forming, ore minerals and gemstones.

*Fossils should be grouped according to whether they're fish, animals or plants.

*Your guide should contain clear, bite-sized facts and good pictures for easy checking.

Fossils

➤ Gastropods
These are commonly known as snails. Their shells are usually coiled in spirals. Their fossils are found in shales, mudstones and limestones formed as far back as 540 million years ago.

Three different kinds of gastropods

➤ Bivalves
These include cockles, mussels and razor shells. Their shells are made of two separate parts, called valves, that are hinged together so the animals inside can open them up to feed and close them for protection. Their fossils are found in shales, limestones and mudstones.

Two different bivalves

56

➤ Brachiopods
Like bivalves, brachiopods have a hinged pair of shells, but the two are a different size and shape, so that one overlaps the other. Their fossils are found in shales, limestones and mudstones, especially those formed between 500 and 285 million years ago.

Some brachiopods' shells have grooves and ridges.

➤ Echinoids (sea urchins)
These are rounded or heart-shaped animals up to 100mm (4in) across. The shell is made of plates of calcite, often covered with lumps. On modern-day sea urchins, spines are attached to these lumps, but the spines are rarely preserved in fossils. Echinoids are found in rocks, especially chalk, that were formed less than 200 million years ago.

Echinoid fossil with lumps, showing where the spines used to be

Heart-shaped echinoid fossil

A modern-day sea urchin with spines

A walk in the country

One of the most enjoyable ways to spot rocks is to go for a walk in the countryside. You don't have to go very far before you'll find yourself surrounded by many kinds of rocks and minerals.

Although much of the landscape may be covered by grass and trees, you'll still find rocks peeking out in exposed places.

Over thousands of years, a river cuts through the rocky landscape, leaving rocks and stones in its banks.

Stone walls built around fields are a useful clue to what type of rock there is in the area.

A waterfall forms if hard rock stops the water from making a deeper channel.

Mountainous areas usually have lots of rocks. The soil is thinner in these places, as it has been gradually washed away by rain.

Moss and lichen

The foot of a cliff is a good place to look for rock fragments and fossils.

Granite is a common rock. Sometimes you'll find huge granite boulders stacked up on top of each other.

Good areas to look are hills and mountains, cliffs and riverbanks, as these are places where it's common to find bare patches of rock. You may come across piles of rocks at the bottom of cliffs too.

WORN AWAY

Granite boulders are the remains of hard igneous rock that has been pushed up under mountains made of a softer rock.

When the mountains have been worn away by wind and rain, the granite is left standing on its own.

Soft rock worn away

WHAT'S SAND MADE OF?

Beach sand is a mixture of rock fragments, a mineral called quartz and pieces of shells from sea creatures. These are ground up by the waves to form sand.

Quartz

Beachcombing

Beaches are good places to study all kinds of rocks, minerals and fossils. Some beaches have a mixture of rocks and sand on them, while others consist of just pebbles.

If you look closely at a sandy beach, you'll find clues about what types of rock the sand is made of. Pale sand contains limestone fragments, and dark sand is made from black volcanic basalt.

Pebbles

Pebbles are shaped by the sea as it batters rock from cliffs and then rolls the pieces around, making them smooth and round. They're easy to pick up and examine, so you can get a close-up view of the types of rocks and minerals in the area.

WATERMARKS

When you pick up a pebble from a beach, it's often wet from the seawater. This helps to show up the patterns so you can identify it more easily.

Rocky beaches can make perfect little fishing ponds for seabirds to feed from.

Most sand is yellow-brown. The shade comes from glassy quartz covered in iron-oxide (rust).

Layers and fossils

Beach cliffs are often striped with different shades of rock, showing how sedimentary rocks have been laid down in layers over millions of years.

You can sometimes find fossils lying on the beach below. These have been weathered out of the cliff face, especially after winter storms.

STRANGERS ON THE SHORE

Not all the rocks and pebbles on a beach are local to the area. Some may have been carried from far away by rivers or glaciers millions of years ago.

Here you can clearly see the bands in the rocks, showing how they were laid down in layers.

Sea stacks are the remains of ancient cliffs worn away by the sea.

WATCH OUT

*Be careful when walking near cliffs as there may be loose rocks. Look out for any signs warning you to keep away, and never go near edges.

*Check with the local tourist office about tide times, and walk on the beach when the tide is going out.

Boulders from the cliff have been washed smooth by the sea.

Look out for fossils in the rocks beneath a cliff.

GETTING CLOSE

A small magnifying lens will help you to look at speckled minerals or fossils in walls.

KEY QUESTIONS

1. What's on the path or pavement you're walking on? Is it made of gravel, stone or concrete slabs?

2. Is there any stone edging to the pavement? If so, it may be made of hard granite.

3. Look at the other houses on the street. Are they all made of the same materials?

4. If not, do you think some of the materials may have been brought in from somewhere else?

5. What's on the roof? Roof materials can change – slate or stone in one area, clay tiles in another.

Towns and gardens

You could look for many kinds of rocky evidence close to home. By looking at the buildings in your town, you may find out about the types of rocks in your area – and you could make a record of your discoveries.

Write down what you see. You may have to do extra research to find out what everything is made of.

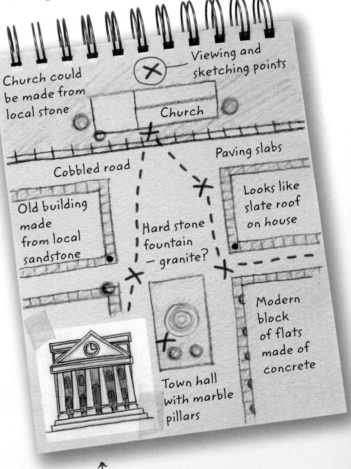

Viewing and sketching points

Church could be made from local stone

Church

Paving slabs

Cobbled road

Old building made from local sandstone

Looks like slate roof on house

Hard stone fountain – granite?

Modern block of flats made of concrete

Town hall with marble pillars

You could make sketches of the buildings and stick them in a notebook.

What's your soil like?

All soil is divided into three main types: acid, alkaline and neutral. The rocks below affect the soil on top. You can find out about the type of soil in your garden or park by measuring its pH (potential of hydrogen) level – this is its acidity or alkalinity.

   You can do this with a simple homemade test. You'll need a small sample of soil, a red cabbage and some paper coffee filters.

FLOWER POWER

Hydrangea flowers change shade depending on the type of soil the plant is growing in. In acidic soils they are blue, in neutral soil they are pale cream, while in alkaline soil they are pink or purple.

Red cabbage

1. Slice the red cabbage into small pieces until you have about 2 cups of chopped cabbage.

2. Place the pieces in a saucepan, cover them with water and simmer for 15 minutes. Allow to cool.

Sieve

3. Strain the cold liquid through a sieve into a bowl. It should be a shade of deep red or purple.

Coffee filter paper

4. Soak a filter paper in the liquid. Allow the paper to dry and then cut it into strips about 2cm (1in) wide.

Stir the mixture

5. Place your soil sample in a plastic bowl. Add some water to it and stir it up into a thick soup.

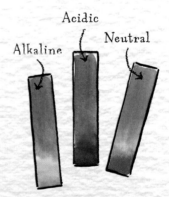

Acidic

Alkaline   Neutral

6. Dip in a paper strip. If it turns green-yellow, the soil is alkaline. If red, acidic. Purple-blue means neutral.

Molten lava pours from a
volcano. This is all part of the
Earth's endless cycle of change.

The restless Earth

The Earth has been changing continuously over millions of years. Sometimes you can see these changes in a dramatic way – when an earthquake splits open the ground, or when a volcano explodes.

But many of the changes take place very, very slowly beneath our feet, unseen and unheard. While up above, on the surface, rocks are being gradually worn and weathered away by wind and water.

A warm heart

Many of the rocks you see around you started life deep inside the Earth, and most of the others have also been affected in some way by heat from the Earth's core.

The core works rather like a huge engine that generates heat. The heat travels out from the core and melts part of the rock in the mantle, which rises up and spreads out. As it spreads, it cools and then sinks back down, and the process begins all over again.

In this diagram you can see the continuous cycle taking place beneath the Earth's surface.

Hot rock (red)rising

Cool rock (blue) sinking

Core

Mantle

Crust

22

Drilling holes

Geologists can only directly study the surface rocks of the crust. Below this, they have to drill holes to collect the rocks. They can't drill any deeper than 16km (10 miles), though, because the heat and pressure would be too great.

Pumice is one of the rocks that shoots out of volcanoes. It is full of tiny holes made by gases.

Blow-outs

During volcanic eruptions, intense heat within the crust and mantle pushes very hot liquid up, and forces it out through cracks in the crust. Boiling rock, thick clouds of ash and poisonous gases are shot into the air and scattered over the surrounding land.

Volcanoes can be extremely destructive, but they can also give geologists a chance to learn a lot more about rocks deep inside the Earth.

This is Kilauea volcano in Hawaii, which has been erupting continuously since 1983.

A NEW ISLAND

There are volcanoes under the sea, as well as on land, and sometimes they can create new islands when they erupt. This happened in 1963 when an eruption off the coast of Iceland forced up a new rocky island named Surtsey.

Our moving world

You might think the Earth's crust would be one solid piece, but it's actually divided into sections, called plates, that fit closely together like parts of a giant jigsaw puzzle. These plates are constantly moving around very slowly, driven along by the heating and cooling process inside the mantle.

The plates often slide, crunch and grind past each other, generating massive friction. Sometimes they push against each other or pull apart. But most of the time we're unaware of any of this.

This diagram shows a view of the Earth with plate boundaries marked in red.

Plate boundaries

Hot mantle

South American plate

24

Mountains and trenches

When two plates in the continental crust push into each other, the crust crumples and folds upward to form fold mountains.

When plates on the ocean floor move apart, magma rises up to fill the gap and sometimes forms underwater mountains called ridges.

When they push against each other, one is forced beneath the other to form a deep trench in the ocean.

Great shakes

Plate boundaries are always cracked and jagged. This means that, as they slide past each other, they can lock together, causing a huge amount of energy to build up. Eventually, one plate is forced to give way and great pulses of energy surge out in the form of an earthquake.

Over a million earthquakes occur every year, but we can't even feel most of them.

The Himalayas in Asia are fold mountains, and the highest mountains in the world.

PUSHING PLATES

When two plates meet head on, one of them has to give way.

On land, one of the plates is forced up and over to form a fold.

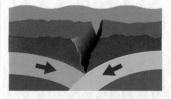

A trench is formed on the ocean floor when one plate is forced down.

Weather and weathering

There is a lot happening on the Earth's surface too. Wind and rain, boiling hot and freezing cold temperatures gradually eat away at the landscape, wearing down and reshaping all the rocks and minerals on the surface. This has been going on ever since the Earth began.

Here are some of the ways it happens.

Frying and freezing

As temperatures rise and fall, rock expands and contracts, making it crack. Rainwater seeps into the cracks, then freezes and expands, shattering the rock.

Weak spots

Some minerals are easily dissolved by water and form weak spots in the rock. If one mineral gives way, others are exposed. Then cracks start to appear and the rock begins to crumble and break up.

Blasted by the wind

Winds full of particles such as sand whip rocky landscapes into shape. This sandblasting wears away the rock surfaces and can form weird and wonderful shapes.

Battered by the sea

*Sea waves can batter rocky headlands, carving out arches. The arches eventually collapse to leave tall sea stacks.

*Weak rocks in the middle of a sea cliff may be worn away by waves to form a cave.

*The rock fragments end up in the sea where they are slowly ground up into sand.

Carried away

*Streams and rivers carry rocks and worn-down fragments toward the sea.

*Slow-moving glaciers creep down mountains, carving out U-shaped valleys and pushing along rocks as they go.

*Rain washes rocky mountain faces smooth.

*In desert areas, gushing water from sudden flash floods can cut deep into soft rocks.

Under the ground

*Weathered and eroded rock is known as sediment and it can build up and harden into layers of sedimentary rock on the ocean floor.

*Where one of the Earth's plates slides beneath another, the sediment is dragged down into the mantle, where it is melted and squeezed. Then the cycle of rock-making begins again.

In this striped sandstone landscape you can see how the rock was laid down, layer upon layer.

Rocks

The Earth is made up from many different rocks, but they can all be divided into one of three types, according to the way they were made.

The most common type is formed by being melted and mixed up in the great bubbling cauldron beneath the Earth's crust. The second type is broken up by wind and water and then laid down in compact layers. The third is created when existing rocks are heated and squeezed so much that they're transformed into new rocks.

Hot rocks

Most rocks are formed when hot, molten rock, called magma, rises up from the mantle and then cools and solidifies. The types of rocks this makes are called igneous rocks.

Intruding rocks

Sometimes, instead of reaching the surface, magma rises up and forces its way – or "intrudes" – between other rocks and hardens inside the Earth's crust. The kind of rock this makes is called "intrusive" igneous rock. Some of this rock only emerges on the surface millions of years later, when the rocks on top have been weathered away. A common example is granite.

At Le Puy in France, an intrusive "plug" of magma hardened inside a volcano. The surrounding rock was worn away, leaving the plug on its own.

The Giant's Causeway in Ireland is made up of columns of extrusive basalt rock that formed as volcanic lava cooled and contracted.

Volcanic rock

The other type of igneous rock is called "extrusive" (meaning "forced out") igneous rock. This forms when the magma, as boiling lava, is forced up through a volcano and onto the Earth's surface, where it cools and hardens. Basalt is a common example.

Lava shoots out of a channel called a pipe. Side pipes form smaller volcanoes.

Extrusive rock hardens over existing rocks.

Intrusions between layers of other rocks are called sills.

The largest igneous intrusions are called batholiths.

Lens-shaped intrusions are called laccoliths.

HOT SPRINGS

The great heat from a volcano not only heats up the surrounding ground – but any water in the ground too. The boiling water sometimes shoots out as hot springs.

Steam from the hot water can be used to power electricity turbines, and minerals in the water and mud can be used in health treatments.

31

Red and brown soil often indicates the presence of iron-rich igneous rocks.

1. Collect some soil and rub it through an old sieve. Rock fragments will be left in the sieve.

2. Empty the fragments, and look at them through a magnifying lens. Can you spot any igneous rocks such as basalt or dolerite?

DID YOU KNOW?

Some of the most fertile soil in the world is found in volcanic areas. This is because it is rich in minerals brought up directly from the Earth's interior.

Igneous rocks to spot

Igneous rocks make up most of the rocks in the Earth's crust. So they're the rocks you will probably find more of when you are out on a collecting expedition.

Here's a selection of some of the most common igneous rocks to look out for – both intrusive and extrusive.

Granite
Common intrusive rock, ranging from white to pink. Mottled because it contains minerals of mica, quartz and feldspar which are easy to spot.

Peridotite
Intrusive rock, varying from fine to coarse. Ranges from dark to light green, and often occurs with metals such as nickel and platinum.

Agglomerate
Extrusive, made of large rounded lumps of volcanic rock such as basalt. May come from pieces of volcanic lava that cooled in the air.

Rhyolite
Extrusive rock, same composition as granite, but with finer grains. Pale or white, but can be reddish or black. Found in volcanic pipes.

Pegmatite
A very coarse intrusive rock with large crystals in it. This makes it easy to study its minerals, mostly feldspar, quartz and mica.

Gabbro
Intrusive igneous rock, coarse-grained with a smooth texture. Formed when magma cools slowly. Dark greenish, speckled with minerals.

Obsidian
Extrusive, natural glass formed when volcanic magma cools quickly. Black and splinters to give sharp edges and smooth surfaces.

Pumice
Extrusive volcanic rock full of gas bubbles made when magma cools quickly. Very light so it can float on water. Pale, often used as an abrasive.

Basalt
Fine- to medium-grained dark extrusive volcanic rock. As the lava cools, it may shrink and crack into six-sided columns. Covers large areas.

Tuff
Made from small pieces of volcanic rock and crystals cemented into hard rock. Extrusive, built up in layers of ash from volcanic explosions.

Dolerite
Also called diabase, a medium-grained intrusive rock, ranging from black to green. One of the most common rocks in the Earth's crust.

Andesite
Common extrusive rock, but only found in volcanic areas on land. Fine-grained and glassy. Often speckled pale green, purple, or brown.

Serpentine
Intrusive, an altered form of peridotite. Mainly composed of the mineral serpentine. Usually dark green, but may have red, green and white stripes.

Layered rocks

Rocks formed in layers are known as sedimentary rocks.

Some sedimentary rocks, such as sandstone, are made from fragments of other rocks. Others, such as limestone, are made from animal remains such as shells, or from chemical crystals and volcanic ash. The fragments, or sediments, are laid down in layers at the bottom of seas, rivers and lakes.

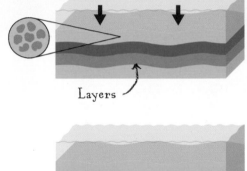

Large and heavy fragments settle first, while smaller and lighter pieces settle more slowly.

Layers

As new sediments settle on the sea floor, their weight presses down on the layers below, making them more compact.

Old layers — New sediments

Limestone landscapes

Limestone is made up mainly of a mineral called calcite, which comes from the shelly remains of tiny sea creatures.

Calcite dissolves easily in rainwater, creating some extraordinary landscapes. Rain eats away at the stone, producing underground caves, towering pinnacles and other amazing shapes.

Limestone

The Grand Canyon

The Grand Canyon in the USA is one of the most spectacular places to see layers of sedimentary rock. It cuts down through nearly 2km (1¼ miles) of sediment to show layers that were laid down over millions of years. The layers range from over 2,000 million years old at the bottom, to about 60 million years old at the top.

The Grand Canyon in Arizona, USA

FINE CHINA

Although it's soft, clay is actually a type of sedimentary rock. The purest clay of all is called kaolin, or china clay, and it's used to make delicate pieces of pottery.

Sedimentary rocks to spot

Sedimentary rocks consist of fragments of rock, seashells and minerals, mixed up and laid down in layers, on the Earth's surface and under the sea.

They're especially valuable to geologists, because the layers can provide a detailed record of the Earth's history. Sedimentary rocks are also the main source of fossils.

Chalk
A very fine-grained type of limestone. Composed of the skeletons of tiny sea animals. Fossils such as sea urchins are often found in it.

Sandstone
Formed of grains of sand – usually from quartz, feldspar and other mineral or rock fragments – under the sea, in rivers and deserts.

Limestone
A common rock, made up mainly of the mineral calcite from the fossil remains of sea creatures. Usually cream, but can also be dark or reddish.

Uluru or Ayers Rock in Australia is an enormous outcrop of sandstone, and it is sacred to the local Aboriginal people.

Conglomerate
Formed from rounded fragments of rock washed down rivers and along coastlines. Fragments of any size, and often have sandy material between.

Stalactites
Found in limestone areas. They hang from the roofs of caves and are formed by the slow dripping of water containing the mineral calcite.

Mudstone and Shale
Formed from hardened sea mud. If the rock parts easily in fine layers it is called shale; if not, it is called mudstone. Black, brown, red or green.

Breccia
Like conglomerate, made of rock fragments set in sandy material. Fragments are angular, showing they were not carried far by water.

Flint
Dark, glassy rock made of chalcedony. Nodules or round lumps often the size of a potato. They separate easily from surrounding rock. Found in chalk.

Tufa
Formed when the mineral calcite hardens out of water around natural springs or hot springs. Has lots of holes and a spongy appearance.

Coal
Black, soft or hard, formed from fossilized plant remains in bogs or swamps. Found in layers, or seams, between other rocks such as sandstone.

Oolite
A type of limestone, made of tiny ball-shaped grains of calcite called ooliths. Yellow, white, sometimes brown. Shells and other fossils often found in it.

Gypsum
Develops when salty water evaporates. Very common. Uniform, fine-grained gypsum, known as alabaster, is soft and often used for carving.

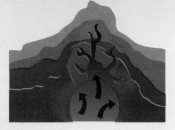

Contact metamorphic rocks usually form near igneous rocks when hot magma heats up the nearby rocks and changes the minerals inside them.

Regional metamorphic rocks are created when the Earth's plates squeeze against each other.

Making new rocks

When igneous or sedimentary rocks are heated and squeezed deep inside the Earth, the minerals inside them are completely changed, forming a new type of rock. This is called metamorphic rock.

This transformation happens in two ways. When rocks are changed by heat alone they're known as "contact" metamorphic rocks.

But when they're changed by great pressure, as well as heat, they're called "regional" metamorphic rocks. Regional metamorphic rocks are the most common of the two types.

Bow Fiddle Sea Stack is an arch of metamorphic quartzite rock on the north east coast of Scotland. It is part of the Caledonian range of fold mountains.

Limestone to marble

One of the best-known metamorphic rocks is marble, which is formed when limestone is heated and squeezed.

If the original limestone is very pure, with no other chemicals in it, the marble will be very white. Impurities produce a marble with stripes of red, yellow, brown, blue or green against a white background.

Quartz into quartzite

Quartzite is a contact metamorphic rock, although it can also be formed by regional metamorphism. It is made from sedimentary sandstone, which consists almost entirely of grains of quartz.

Extreme heat changes the quartz grains into a mass of interlocking crystals, forming quartzite. Quartzite is very hard and you can often see it on exposed hillsides, in riverbanks and road cuttings.

Marble with impurities can produce beautiful decorative building stone.

MARBLE MAHAL

Some of the world's most beautiful buildings, including the Taj Mahal in India and the Parthenon in Athens, are made from marble. Some marble is softer than others and is easily eroded by wind, rain and pollution.

Quartz is the main ingredient of quartzite, sometimes mixed with other minerals such as feldspar and mica.

It is very unusual to find any pebbles or fossils inside metamorphic rocks. This is because the heat and pressure involved in making metamorphic rock is so great that the shapes of the pebbles and fossils are either changed or destroyed.

The pebbles in this stone have been squeezed into ovals.

This fossil of a trilobite has been squeezed out of shape.

The Parthenon temple in Athens was built of marble by the Greeks about 2,500 years ago.

Metamorphic rocks to spot

Metamorphic rocks are formed when igneous or sedimentary rocks are changed by heat and pressure, or by heat alone. They are some of the most interesting rocks to look at, because you can often clearly see the mixture of rocks they are made up from, in the form of stripes and swirling patterns. Here are some common examples of metamorphic rocks.

Gneiss
Formed by heat and pressure. Coarse-grained and consists mostly of the minerals feldspar, mica and quartz, arranged in irregular (wavy) bands.

Marble
Mainly made of the mineral calcite. Formed by heat or pressure on limestone. Common, and can be found in mountain areas all over the world.

Mica schist
Schists are fine-grained, layered rocks from mudstone and siltstone. Mica schist contains the mineral mica, making it dark or silvery.

Garnet schist
Similar to mica schist, but also contains garnets. Rounded in shape, varying in size and often dark red, green or white. Splits easily.

Quartzite
Consists mainly of grains of quartz, but can contain feldspar, mica or other minerals. Made of metamorphosed quartz sandstone. Often white.

Amphibolite
A medium- to coarse-grained rock, mostly of hornblende and feldspar. Formed from igneous rocks such as basalt. Dark with pale bands.

Steatite
Also known as soapstone, created by heat and pressure. Largely consists of mineral talc. Slightly slippery to touch, hence its name. Soft, easy to carve.

Phyllite
Formed from shale and mudstone. Created under great heat and pressure. Green, pale or silvery, with a shiny surface. Splits easily.

Slate
Formed when shale and mudstone are heated and squeezed. Consists of tiny grains of minerals such as mica. Black, red, green or purple. Splits easily.

Skarn
Formed from limestone in contact with granite. Found in northern Europe, Japan and USA, it is often a source of iron and copper.

Migmatite
A mixed rock that is part metamorphic and part igneous. The two components occur in very irregular bands. Makes an attractive building stone.

HARD PRINTS

Cement is a building material made from crushed limestone. You can use it to make your own hand prints.

1. Empty a small bag of cement into a bucket. Slowly add water a little at a time, following the instructions on the bag.

2. Stir the mixture each time you add water, until it becomes smooth and firm. Pour it onto a tray with raised edges.

3. Spread it out evenly. Wearing rubber gloves, press your hands onto it. Leave it for a day and your prints will be set hard.

Using rocks

People have been using rocks as materials for building and as tools for making things for hundreds of thousands of years. We've dug and blasted them out of the ground, cut them into pieces and crushed them into powder. And, by doing all this, we've changed the landscape too.

The first tools

One of the very first rocks to be used as a tool was flint. Flint is a hard, glassy stone found in potato-sized lumps called nodules, and it can be chipped to form sharp edges for cutting and piercing. Some of the earliest flint tools found are about 700,000 years old.

Flint was used by early people to make knives, spears, axes and arrowheads. Other rocks, such as granite and limestone, were chipped and shaped into tools such as grinding stones and hammers.

Softer stones, such as marble and alabaster, are much easier to cut and carve. So they were rubbed and polished with sand to make sculptures.

This flint hand axe was made about 250,000 years ago and it would have been used to chop up meat for eating.

Painting with rocks

More than 20,000 years ago, early artists decorated the walls of caves using paints made from crushed rocks, clays, chalk, earth and charcoal with animal fat and water. Some rocks are still used to make paints today.

The caves at Lascaux in France were decorated about 17,000 years ago using paints made from rocks.

PAINT STONES

Here are some stones used to make paints.

Lapis lazuli - blue

Malachite - green

Cinnabar - red

Building stones

The first homes were made of grasses and even animal bones and skins. But once people had the tools to dig and cut rocks, they started using stone instead.

Man-made building materials such as bricks, cement and glass are also made from crushed rocks and minerals.

The Egyptian pyramids were built nearly 5,000 years ago from huge limestone blocks.

Quartz crystals growing
inside a hollow ball of
rock called a geode

Minerals

Rocks are what we see on the surface, but look inside them and you'll find a whole world of minerals in all kinds of shapes and shades.

Many minerals play a starring role in our everyday lives, from the razzle dazzle of precious stones to the metals and other materials that we all depend on.

Mineral building blocks

Minerals are the building blocks of rocks.
Although there are thousands of different
minerals, only a few hundred of these are
common ingredients in rocks. Some of them
are the source of materials we use every day,
but many more are very rare and valuable.

Crystal power

Minerals are made up of simple chemical
substances called elements, such as oxygen,
silicon, iron and calcium. Most of them come
in the form of little blocks called crystals, that
lock together to form hard, solid rock.
    Some of the best crystals are found in hollow
balls of rock called geodes. Hot gases or liquids
seep in and crystallize as they cool.

You may be lucky enough
to find a geode. If you
crack it open like
an egg, you'll find
crystals inside.

Diamonds are sometimes found in a volcanic rock known as kimberlite.

This diamond has been cut and polished. A diamond in its natural state is shown above.

Native elements

Most minerals are made up of two or more elements but a few, like diamond, consist of just one. These are called native elements.

Diamonds grow when the element carbon is heated and squeezed inside the upper mantle of the Earth. They can sometimes be carried to the surface during volcanic eruptions.

Identifying minerals

Most mineral crystals have a regular shape or structure. This gives geologists important clues to help them to identify the minerals in rocks. You can find out more about crystals and their shapes on the next page.

STREAK TEST

If you want to identify a mineral you've found, try this simple test.

1. Place a tile, such as a bathroom tile, face down, so that the rough side is facing upward.

2. Take your mineral and rub it across the tile. It should leave a line or streak behind it.

3. Compare the streak with the mineral descriptions in your field guide.

Dark red streak — could be hematite

Crystal patterns

One of the things that makes crystals special is that they all come in regular, or symmetrical, shapes. For example, for every side or "face" on a crystal, there is another face on the other side of the crystal that is parallel to it.

This is because the different elements in a mineral always group together in the same proportion. The elements form simple patterns, and the pattern is always the same in any particular mineral. This helps geologists to identify them.

REGULAR SHAPES

Many minerals can be identified by their shapes. If you look closely at a crystal and can count the number of sides, or faces, it has, and at what angle they meet, it'll help you to identify what family it belongs to.

Here are some typical crystal shapes.

Cubic

Monoclinic

Hexagonal

Rhombic

Tetragonal   Triclinic

Even though these quartz crystals are growing in different directions, each one has parallel faces.

Grow your own crystals

You can grow your own crystals, either using a kit from a hobby shop or some table salt from the kitchen. You'll also need a glass jar, some hot water, a pencil, a piece of string, a paperclip and a metal spoon.

HANDY HINT

If you don't have any salt, try using baking soda or sugar instead. To make brighter crystals, you could also add a drop of food dye or ink to the water.

The spoon will protect the jar by preventing the hot water from cracking the glass.

1. Place the spoon in the jar. Then slowly pour in hot water so that it's about three-quarters full.

Some salt will stay at the bottom of the jar.

2. Add the salt slowly and keep stirring until no more will dissolve. This is called a saturated solution.

The string should be long enough so the paperclip can hang in the middle of the jar.

3. Tie the string to the middle of a pencil, and then tie the paperclip to the other end of the string.

4. Lower the paperclip into the jar, resting the pencil on top. Then leave the jar for a couple of days.

5. After a day, you'll see salt crystals forming on the string and the paperclip and at the water surface.

Salt crystals are also called halite crystals. They are found in sedimentary rocks in lumps, or as single cubic crystals.

Making minerals

Many of the Earth's minerals can be found in a whole range of different rocks – igneous, sedimentary and metamorphic. But some minerals are usually only found in just one type of rock.

Minerals in igneous rocks

Many minerals develop directly inside the magma as igneous rocks are forming. Others develop when gases escape from the magma and a reaction takes place with the rock next to it, or as the magma cools.

Minerals created like this are known as igneous minerals. They include some of the more common minerals, such as feldspars, micas and quartz.

Feldspar is one of the main minerals in this volcanic basalt rock.

New minerals

Some new "metamorphic" minerals develop when minerals in rocks go through chemical changes. This happens during the metamorphic process, when the rocks are pulled down into deeper parts of the Earth's crust and heated and squeezed.

Garnet is an example of a metamorphic mineral. It is found in many metamorphic rocks, such as gneisses and schists, and can range from dark red and pink to brown and bright green. The finest garnet crystals are used as gemstones (see page 54).

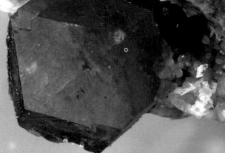

A bright pink garnet crystal set in quartz and calcite

Other minerals

Some minerals develop when rocks on the Earth's surface are weathered by water and chemicals. Common examples are members of the clay mineral group, such as kaolinite and chlorite. Others, such as calcite which makes up limestone, are formed as the hard parts of animals. Still others, such as gypsum and halite, form as salty water evaporates.

TURQUOISE

Turquoise is a pale blue sedimentary mineral formed when water reacts with rocks that contain aluminium (aluminum). The best turquoise comes from Iran, where it has been mined for over 3,000 years.

Gypsum

Calcite

Halite

Polished turquoise

Turquoise fragment

51

Rock-forming minerals

There are about 3,500 known minerals, and scientists discover about 20 new ones every year. But only a small number of these make up nearly all of the rocks in the Earth's crust.

The most common minerals of all belong to the huge silicate family. There are about 1,000 different types of silicate, including quartz, which also comes in many different varieties.

Fluorite
Also called fluorspar, forms cube-shaped crystals. Blue, purple, green or yellow. Glows in ultra-violet light, creating fluorescence.

Halite
Also known as rock salt, this is the salt we eat. Transparent or white in its purest form, but usually stained brown or yellow. Tastes salty.

Apatite
Mined from rocks for use as a fertilizer. Your teeth are also made mostly of apatite, and so are your bones. Pale green, blue-green, white or brown.

Baryte
Fairly common, crystals tend to be white, but sometimes tinged yellow, brown or red. Often glassy-looking and clear. Heavy to hold.

Augite
Short, fat column-shaped crystals with eight sides. Black to dark green. Augite is mainly found in basalt and other types of igneous rocks.

Gypsum
Crystals found in prisms, needles or tabular plates. Can be white, but clear pieces were once used as a form of glass. Scratches with fingernail.

Milky quartz
The most common variety of quartz, and easily found. Opaque, white. Found as crystals or small lumps. All quartzes are part of the silicate family.

Mica
Two main types: biotite is black or brown and shiny, and muscovite is white and silvery. Both have thin flakes, and are common in granites.

Talc
The softest mineral, made of silicon, magnesium, oxygen and hydrogen. Pale green, but can be white. Easily crushed, used in talcum powder.

Calcite
Made of calcium, carbon and oxygen. White, but can be green, yellow or blue. Six-sided shapes, forms "fur" inside kettles. Scratches with knife.

Feldspar
Made up of a variety of elements, feldspars are easily found in many igneous rocks. Six-sided crystals, ranging from white to pale pink.

Rock crystal
A type of quartz, clear and transparent. Found as crystals or small lumps. Sometimes mistaken for diamonds. Used to make decorative objects.

Olivine
Made of magnesium, iron, silicon and oxygen. Usually forms grainy masses and often olive green, but some white or black. Weathers to brown.

Hornblende
Consists of many different elements. Large crystals, green or black. Found in a wide range of both igneous and metamorphic rocks, especially amphibolite.

Some gemstones, known as birthstones, have been dedicated to the months of the years. You can match the month of your birthday to a particular gem.

 January : garnet

 February : amethyst

 March : aquamarine

 April : diamond

 May : emerald

 June : pearl

 July : ruby

 August : peridot

 September : sapphire

 October : opal

 November : topaz

December : turquoise

Gemstones

Some crystals are especially prized for their sparkling beauty, rarity and value. They are known as precious gemstones. The stars in the mineral family, they're cut and polished to make spectacular jewels for rings, earrings and necklaces.

Some minerals come in different varieties, producing more than one type of gem. Their different shades are caused by metal impurities in the mineral mix.

Top of the rocks

About 20 of the precious gemstones are the most prized of all, because they are the rarest and most beautiful.

At the top of the list is the diamond, with its flashing fire. Other important ones include red ruby and blue sapphire – both varieties of the mineral corundum – and emerald, which is a grass green form of the mineral beryl.

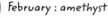

Most diamonds are clear. But some, known as "fancy" diamonds, are yellow, pink, blue or even brown and black. This is a fancy pink diamond.

Aquamarine crystals are named after "sea water" because their shade is a pale blue-green.

A sparkling family

The mineral beryl comes in different varieties, from pink and yellow to green emerald and pale blue aquamarine. The different shades are caused by tiny amounts of chromium in emerald and iron in aquamarine.

Decorative minerals

There are less valuable minerals that are described as semi-precious gemstones. But they can also be very beautiful, and they're easier to find and collect than precious stones.

Semi-precious minerals were first used to make jewels and decorative objects by the ancient Egyptians, Sumerians and Chinese thousands of years ago. Some of the best known are carnelian, turquoise, lapis lazuli and jade.

COLLECTING

Minerals can make a beautiful display.

1. Clean stones in water, using an old toothbrush to remove any mud.

2. Try to identify each one when you've finished cleaning it.

3. Place them in a box with labels and padding to prevent any chipping.

LIVING JEWELS

There are other types of precious gems, which come from animals. Red and black coral is highly prized and carved into jewels. Pearls from oysters have been collected for thousands of years – the most valuable are huge pearls from the South Pacific islands.

Pearl

Precious gemstones to spot

Bright and beautiful, gemstones range from dazzling precious stones, such as diamonds and emeralds, to semi-precious stones such as amethyst and lapis lazuli.

The value of gemstones changes as fashions change. Diamonds and rubies have kept their value for thousands of years. But other stones once considered precious may be less so today. Here are some well-known precious gems.

Spinel
Looking like a ruby, the most prized is blood red. Other shades are pink, blue and yellow. Usually forms as small, eight-sided crystals.

Spinel

Opal
Made of silicon, oxygen and water. Milky white to a mixture of blue, red and yellow. The most precious is black opal, with more flash and fire.

Polished opal

Ruby
A variety of the mineral corundum. Only red crystals are called rubies. The most expensive shade is called "pigeon's blood" red, found in Myanmar.

Cut rubies

Sapphire
Another type of corundum. The most prized is deep blue, but can also be pink or yellow. The most valuable stones are found in Kashmir.

Diamond
The hardest mineral of all, it is made of carbon. Occurs in volcanic kimberlite. Often clear, but also yellow, red, blue, brown, even black.

Cut diamond

Peridot
This is the gem variety of the mineral olivine. Occurs in igneous rocks and ranges from pale to olive green. Very popular in the early 20th century.

Tourmaline
Long crystals with parallel lines along their length. Often black, but blue, green and pink shades also occur, sometimes together.

Emerald
A member of the beryl family, this can be one of the most valuable gemstones. Grass green stones from Colombia are considered the best.

Aquamarine
Another member of the beryl family. Its pale blue-green shade comes from tiny amounts of iron mixed with the mineral. Main source: Brazil.

Imperial topaz
Topaz is usually classed as a semi-precious stone, but the rich golden shade of imperial topaz makes it rare and highly prized. Hard but easily broken.

Cut topaz

Zircon
Sometimes mistaken for diamond. Formed from zirconium silicate, in a range of shades caused by different impurities. Mined in Sri Lanka.

Chrysoberyl
Very hard yellow-green gemstone, exceeded in hardness only by diamond and corundum. A variety called alexandrite changes from green to red in light.

Tanzanite
A blue variety of the mineral zoisite. Crystals are found in gneisses in northern Tanzania. Rich blue, purple and green shades at different angles.

Semi-precious gemstones

You'll probably never be lucky enough to find a precious stone when you're out collecting, but there are lots of semi-precious stones that will look good in your collection.

Good places to search are beaches, where you can sometimes find semi-precious stones in the sand and among other pebbles. Here are some of the best-known examples.

Chalcedony
A member of the quartz family. Fine-grained and doesn't form crystals. It is a porous (absorbent) stone, which means it can be dyed various shades.

Lapis lazuli
Found in Afghanistan and made of minerals including sodalite and calcite. A deep blue, used for thousands of years as a decorative stone.

Smoky quartz
Sometimes known as cairngorm, it forms transparent six-sided crystals. Ranges from a shade of smoky-brown to nearly black.

Amethyst
Another type of quartz, deep purple to pale blue. A popular semi-precious stone used in jewels. Found as crusts lining geodes in volcanic rocks.

Carnelian
A member of the chalcedony family, this ranges from red to brown-red. Has been used to make jewels for thousands of years.

Polished carnelian

Agate
A type of quartz, it is made up of shaded bands. Most agate occurs in rounded lumps. The middle may form a geode with rock crystals inside.

Rhodonite
Bright pink or red caused by manganese, with black flecks and veins. Crystals in tabular plates, found in schists. Used as a decorative stone.

Tiger's-eye
Another member of the chalcedony family. It is composed of tiny fibrous lines that reflect the light, hence its name. Black with gold stripes.

Garnet
A mixture of various elements, it comes in many different varieties. Common dark red to rarer bright green. Found in some metamorphic rocks.

Cut garnet

Topaz
Contains various minerals mixed with water and fluorine. Large crystals ranging from clear to brown, pink and blue. Popular as jewels.

Nephrite
Sometimes called jade, but a different mineral from jadeite. White or green, made of interlocking grains, making it tough. Popular as a carved stone.

Jadeite
A semi-precious stone found as pebbles or rocks in streams. Shades include milky white, but the most valuable is a bright green highly prized in China.

Turquoise
Made mainly of copper, aluminium (aluminum) and phosphorus. Usually found in hot, dry regions once covered in water. Sky blue to apple green.

Polished turquoise

Minerals and metals

Metals are some of the most important materials we get from inside the Earth. Most metals are found as ores – minerals that contain metal combined with elements such as oxygen or carbon.

Copper and gold were the first metals to be used – about 6,000 years ago – to make tools and jewels. They're easier to work than other metals as they're often found in a pure form, not mixed with other substances.

Iron wasn't used until about 3,000 years later, as a lot of heat is needed to extract it from the ore.

This lump of quartz has veins of pure gold in it. The gold can be easily extracted by crushing and then heating the rock.

This gold mask from ancient Greece is about 3,500 years old.

Everyday uses

Metals have an amazing range of properties. They are strong and long-lasting and can be beaten into thin flat sheets or drawn out to make wire. Some can be mixed with others to create new metals called alloys.

We have been using metals ever since people first discovered that a glinting piece of copper could be made into a tool. Today, you can find them in practically everything, from aircraft and cars to mobile phones and computers.

Hematite

Chalcopyrite

Metals in industry

Iron, copper and lead are among the most important metals used in industry today. Hematite is the main mineral ore for iron, while chalcopyrite produces copper and galena is the main ore for lead.

Gold, silver and platinum are precious metals, but they're also important in industry too, especially in the oil refining and electronics industries.

Galena

Here, molten steel is being poured from a furnace. Steel is made by blasting air through molten iron.

Ore minerals to spot

The most valuable and useful minerals are the ore minerals. Ores contain metals, such as iron, zinc, lead and copper, which are mined, then crushed and heated (known as smelting) to extract the metals inside. The metals are then refined and processed and used to make all sorts of things that we use every day.

COMMON METALS

Metals are found in many ore minerals, but only about 100 of these are worth the cost of mining them. The most common metals are aluminium (aluminum), iron, potassium, calcium, sodium and magnesium.

Fireworks contain magnesium.

Cinnabar
Red with small crystals. Mostly granular, occurs in sedimentary and volcanic rocks. The source of the fluid metal mercury. Streak: red.

Arsenopyrite
Made of sulphur (sulfur), iron and arsenic. Also called mispickel. Often found with gold and quartz. Streak: black.

Stibnite
Also known as antimonite, the main source of the rare metal antimony. The crystals have a dull shine. Also found with lead and silver. Streak: pale.

Orpiment
This has small crystals, ranging from lemon to orange with a pearly shine. A source of arsenic, once used in yellow paints. Streak: yellow.

Gold
An unmixed element. Found as specks, but sometimes as small lumps called nuggets in igneous and sedimentary rocks. Streak: gold.

Silver
Can be found as small specks and wiry shapes in igneous rocks. Silver-white, but quickly tarnishes (goes black) in air. Streak: silver-white.

Pyrite
Contains iron and sulphur. Known as iron pyrites or fool's gold, due to its appearance. Many fossils contain pyrite. Streak: green-black.

Chalcopyrite
One of the main sources of copper. This mineral is found in igneous and metamorphic rocks. Brass yellow, but tarnishes. Streak: green-black.

Galena
Made of lead and sulphur. Cubic crystals found in sedimentary rocks. When freshly split it is silvery, but tarnishes. Streak: silver-black.

Malachite
Made of copper, carbon, oxygen and hydrogen. Copper produces the light and dark green bands. Used as an ornamental stone. Streak: pale green.

Hematite
Contains iron and oxygen, and found in sedimentary rocks. Also known as kidney ore. Shade from steel to black. Streak: red-brown.

Magnetite
Contains iron and oxygen, like hematite, but in different proportions. Very magnetic, it forms small black crystals. Streak: black.

Sphalerite
Also known as zinc blende, it is the most important source of zinc. It occurs with galena and varies from brown, yellow to black. Streak: brown.

This amazing fossil is of a
crocodile-like reptile called
a Mesosaurus. The entire
skeleton can be clearly seen.

Fossils

Fossils are the preserved remains of animals and plants that lived on Earth a very long time ago.

When you look at a fossil, you are staring directly at a moment in time that has been captured, sometimes hundreds of millions of years ago. Fossils can tell us things about a time when the Earth was completely different, and they can also provide us with glimpses into the future.

What are fossils?

If the remains of an animal or plant are buried quickly by sediments such as mud or sand, there is a good chance that they will be fossilized. Then, after thousands of years, a rock hard impression will form, known as a fossil.

Most fossils are found in rocks that once lay beneath the sea, where sediments were laid down all the time. So it's much more common to find fossils of shells and corals than fossils of land animals and birds.

Hard pieces of an animal or plant do sometimes survive, like the pearly shell of this ammonite fossil.

How are fossils formed?

Most fossils are the remains of the hard parts of animals and plants, such as shells, skeletons and wood. The soft parts usually decay, or are eaten, so it's only the remains that are left that are buried under sediment. The sediments press down and harden. At the same time, water washes through the remains, filling up the pores and cavities with minerals and fossilizing them in the rock.

When did this happen?

Thousands, millions and hundreds of millions of years ago. Sedimentary rocks containing fossils were laid down in layers known as strata. The prehistoric period has been divided up into different ages, or eras, named after sets of strata that contain similar fossils.

The oldest fossils ever found are those of simple organisms, such as bacteria and algae, that lived over 3,500 million years ago. Larger organisms, such as trilobites, appeared more recently – 570 million years ago.

Trilobites were small sea creatures with hard, scaly bodies. They can often be found fossilized.

PAST ERAS

*Precambrian - from the birth of our Earth, about 4,600 million years ago.

*Paleozoic - between 570 million and 245 million years ago.

*Mesozoic - between 245 million and 65 million years ago.

*Cenozoic - from 65 million years ago to the present time.

Can we date them?

Scientists use various ways of dating rocks where fossils are found. Some of these are based on something that's very common in the natural world: radioactive decay. Two of these methods – fission-track dating and potassium-argon dating – can record dates going back millions of years. When scientists know the age of the rocks, they can work out the age of any fossils inside them.

OLD BONES

Geologists have used the potassium-argon method to date rocks at sites in East Africa, such as Olduvai Gorge, which contain fossils of early human ancestors.

WHICH IS IT?

Fossils come in different types. Look for the following:

Imprint   Cast

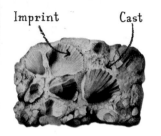

The impression of the outside of a fossil in the rock in which it was formed is called an imprint.

If an imprint is filled with new material, it forms a fossil-like object called a cast.

When a plant or animal is dissolved by water and minerals have replaced the body, it is called a replacement fossil.

This fossil of an ancient fish clearly shows its bony skeleton and spiky tail and fins.

Classifying fossils

Scientists who study fossils are called palaeontologists, and they group fossils in the same way that biologists group living things today – as fish, animals and plants.

Fish fossil   Animal fossil   Plant fossil

Fishy fossils

Some of the oldest and most common fossils are the remains of creatures that lived on the sea bed, where sand and mud settled in layers. This meant their remains were quickly covered and fossilized.

As hard parts are the most easily preserved, sea creatures with shells and some fish with skeletons and thick scales have been found.

Animals and birds

Animals and birds have lived on Earth for millions of years, but fossils of their remains are fairly rare. This is because, although bone is hard, it is easily destroyed by chemical processes in the soil.

A few complete fossil skeletons of animals such as dinosaurs have been found, but mostly in areas that were once covered with water. It's more common to find fossilized teeth, because they're much harder-wearing than bones.

These are fossil skeletons of sea lizards called Mosasaurs.

They weren't dinosaurs, but they lived about 200 million years ago, at the same time as dinosaurs roamed the land.

Trees and plants

Fossils of trees and plants are fairly common because they develop tough trunks and branches. Fossilized leaves, branches, bark, seeds, roots and even whole tree trunks have been found. Some of the oldest known tree fossils belong to a tree called a Ginkgo that dates back 245 million years. This type of tree still grows today.

HUMAN FOOTPRINTS

In 1976, the 4 million year-old fossil footprints of two early human ancestors were found in Tanzania. The footprints were pressed into soft ash, which hardened and was covered with more ash and mud.

Seashells and corals
have been found on
the tops of hills.

Looking for fossils

Knowing where to look is the most important
part of being a fossil hunter. The best way
to find out which are the good sites to visit
is to talk to someone who knows them and
can show you around. Many local geological
societies and museums organize trips.

Cliffs and quarries

Riverbanks and cliffs eroded by the sea are
good sites for fossil hunters. You can often
find fossils in rocks that have fallen down.

Limestone cliffs are some of the best places
of all. Rocks exposed on hilltops, in stone
quarries and in road and railway cuttings are
also good places to look.

Rock now at the top of a hill may once
have been on the ocean floor. The
movement of the Earth's plates gradually
pushed rocks with fossils up to the top.

Remains of coral
in the rock

Fossil shells of sea
creatures called
ammonites

Sometimes you can
find fossils in the most
surprising places.

Watery graves

Even areas that are now desert may
contain fossils – if that area was once
covered by water. A good place to look
for fossils is in shale rock formed from sea
mud, and in rocks containing coal that were
laid down in watery places such as lakes,
marshes and river estuaries.

Crinoids, or
sea lilies, lived on
the sea floor about
500 million years ago.

A sticky end

The fossilized resin from pine trees, known
as amber, sometimes contains the remains of
whole insects such as spiders and flies. These
became trapped in the sticky resin and were
preserved and fossilized. Even small animals
such as frogs and lizards have been found
preserved in this way.

This fly got stuck in
pine resin millions of
years ago and the resin
fossilized into amber.

Fossil of a sea
snail called a
gastropod

These are shark's
teeth that fossilized
about 200 million
years ago.

FROZEN IN TIME
The complete bodies
of an ancient type
of elephant called a
mammoth have been
found preserved in
the frozen ground
of Siberia in Russia.
Even the mammoths'
hair and skin
have survived.

Fossil fuels

Fossils can have much more practical uses too. Most of the fuels we use – in the form of oil, gas and coal – come from the fossilized remains of animals and plants. For this reason, they're sometimes called fossil fuels.

Ancient energy

Coal is formed over millions of years from the remains of trees and plants that once grew in freshwater swamps. When they died, layers of sand and clay gradually settled on top and the remains were slowly changed by chemical processes. They were then compressed into thick, underground layers, or seams, of hard coal running between the layers of sedimentary rock.

Coal

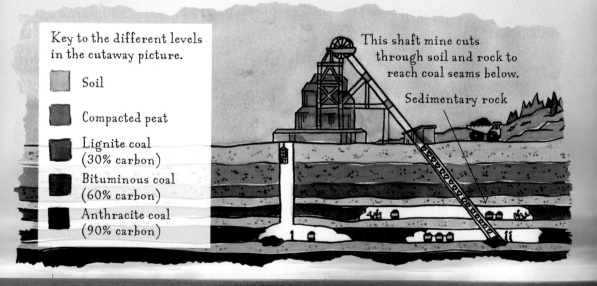

Key to the different levels in the cutaway picture.

Soil

Compacted peat

Lignite coal (30% carbon)

Bituminous coal (60% carbon)

Anthracite coal (90% carbon)

This shaft mine cuts through soil and rock to reach coal seams below.

Sedimentary rock

Oil is formed from the remains of tiny sea creatures, and gas from the remains of land plants as well as sea creatures. These fuels are fluid, rather than solid, and become trapped underground in large pools or reservoirs within the rocks.

Mining and drilling

The coal we use comes from underground mines, or opencast mines (huge open holes dug in the ground).

Oil was first drilled on land, but as more oil is needed so the search for it has also spread into the sea. To extract oil and gas, a drill, supported by a structure called a rig, bores a hole into the ground or seabed.

These are magnified microfossils in rocks. Oil geologists use them to date the rocks.

Oil rig in the North Sea, lying off the coast of Scotland

DIAMOND TIPS

For its size, the most expensive part of a drilling rig is the diamond-tipped "bit". This is used to drill through very hard rocks to reach the reservoirs of oil and gas inside them.

Drill bit

What fossils can tell us

Most scientists today believe that the Earth was formed about 4,600 million years ago. By studying its rocks and the fossils they contain, we are gradually finding out more about the Earth's history. Even the tiniest remains can reveal the most fascinating information.

Early life

The earliest forms of life were very simple bacteria. Then, about 600 million years ago, more complex animals began to appear on land and there was an explosion of new life.

This process of change is known as evolution. Thousands of plants and animals have become extinct, but we know what they looked like from their fossil remains.

Here are some of the sea creatures that started appearing about 550 million years ago. Many of them have been discovered as fossils.

Trilobites hunted for food on sea floor.

Sponge coral

Straight cone nautiloid

Brachiopods had shells on stalks from the ground.

Sea lilies caught food with their wavy arms.

The oldest fossils

The oldest fossils that have been found all show extremely simple forms of life, such as bacteria and algae. Some of these date back to around 3,500 million years ago. Similar forms of life can still be found today.

Some bacteria fossils, like these, are 3,500 million years old.

Fossil clues

Most fossils show the bones, teeth or shells of prehistoric creatures, and palaeontologists can learn a lot about an animal from these clues.

For example, the size and width of bones can give an idea of what the creature looked like, its size and weight. The shape of an animal's teeth can indicate the kind of food – whether meat or plants – that it could chew.

This fossil of a Triceratops suggests it snipped leaves with its beak-like mouth.

SURPRISE FIND

Scientists thought the Coelacanth fish had died out 65 million years ago. So they were amazed when a living one was found off South Africa in 1938.

Ammonites moved by pumping air through their hollow shells.

Starfish

Bryozoans formed a lacy network of tiny tubes.

Pie-shaped coral

The past and the future

Fossil remains can also provide glimpses into the future of the Earth. Satellites monitor the Earth's climate all the time, but scientists can only decide if conditions are normal or not by working out what climates were like in the past. Fossils can give them clues about this, and what the future might hold.

Satellite pictures like this one are used to predict rain or droughts across the world. Warm rain clouds are shown in pink.

225 million years ago

135 million years ago

65 million years ago

Today

Drifting apart

Scientists believe that the world's continents were once all joined together. This is because fossils of the same kinds of animals and plants, and from the same period, have been found on both sides of an ocean.

For example, fossils in the Caledonian mountains of northern Europe are identical to ones found in the Appalachian mountains of North America. Africa and North America were also joined together millions of years ago. The fossil remains of Ceratosaurus dinosaurs have been found both in Tendaguru in East Africa and in Utah in North America.

Climate change

The Earth's climate has changed over millions of years.

Plant fossils found in the freezing Arctic and Antarctica, where few plants and animals can live now, show that these areas once had a warm climate and were covered in plants and trees.

Fossil corals can provide clues about sea temperatures millions of years ago, while living corals can tell us about how the climate is changing today.

Seed fern fossil

Horsetail fossil

Club moss fossil

The Arctic region was once covered with lush plants, like this fern fossilized in stone.

The world in the future

With the information they have gathered from fossils and rocks, and using satellites that monitor the movement of the Earth's plates, scientists try to calculate what the world will look like millions of years ahead.

They predict that the Atlantic Ocean will probably keep on opening up, while the Pacific Ocean will close. Australia will continue to move north until it collides with Southeast Asia. China will split in half and mountain ranges will be pushed up all over the world.

MINI MESSAGES
Even fossils of the smallest creatures of all, known as microfossils, can provide vital information to help scientists understand more about what the world's climate used to be like.

YOUNG HUNTER

One of the youngest fossil hunters was 11 year-old Mary Anning. She discovered her first fossil in 1810 on the south coast of England near where she lived. It was of a prehistoric sea creature called an Icthyosaur. She made many more important fossil discoveries.

Icthyosaur

Fossils from the sea to spot

The most common fossils to find are those of plants and animals that once lived in the sea and other watery areas. Some fossils, such as those of corals and sea urchins, are very common because they have existed for hundreds of millions of years.

Fossils from the sea can be some of the most interesting to collect, because they come in so many different shapes and sizes.

Fossil fish
Fish have hard parts such as skeletons, bony fins and tails and thick scales that are sometimes fossilized. But finding these is quite rare.

Corals
Simple animals with skeletons made of calcite. Fossils often found on their own or in groups called colonies. Oldest are 510 million years old.

Belemnites
Looked a little like modern squids. The fossils are the remains of hard internal parts. Bullet-shaped with pointed end, about 10cm (4in) long.

Crinoids
Also known as sea lilies, because of their long bodies and arms. Common fossils in hard limestones. Related to sea urchins and starfish.

Ammonites
Small sea creatures that used air inside their shells to float. Fossils are flat spirals found in rocks formed 245 to 65 million years ago.

Echinoids
Sea urchin fossils with rounded shells up to 10cm (4in) across. Found in rocks, especially chalk, formed less than 450 million years ago.

Brachiopods
Like bivalves, they have a hinged pair of shells, but a different shape. Fossils in shales, limestones and mudstones less than 550 million years old.

Bivalves
Includes cockles, mussels and razor shells. Their shells are in two parts, which the animals open to feed. Fossils found in shales and limestones.

Trilobites
Creatures with body segments, but only head and tail fossils usually found. In siltstones and mudstones between 550 and 250 million years old.

Trace fossils
A fossil made not from the creature itself, but the tracks of its movements in the sand. These can reveal information about the creature that made them.

Fish teeth
Fossil fish bones are rare but their teeth are quite common. Teeth from rays and sharks have been found in rocks up to 400 million years old.

Gastropods
Commonly known as snails. Shells usually spiral. Fossils found in shales, mudstones and limestones up to 540 million years old.

Starfish
Members of the echinoderm family, which includes crinoids and sea urchins. Found in rocks, such as limestone, up to 500 million years old.

Fossils show us just how much plants and animals have changed over millions of years. But some of the earliest plants can still be found today.

For example, horsetail grasses date back 400 million years, while the monkey puzzle tree dates back about 245 million years.

Plant and animal fossils

While the fossils of sea creatures are fairly easy to find, the fossils of land animals and birds are less common. This is because their remains rotted away or were eaten by other animals long before they could be covered up and preserved under layers of soil. But you can sometimes find the fossilized leaves and other parts of land plants.

Fossil wood
The original wood of ancient trees turns to carbon (coal), or may be replaced by minerals dissolved in water. Growth rings can be preserved.

Whole animals
Whole bodies of animals have been found preserved in frozen ground, and other animals have been found preserved in tar pits.

These fossilized footprints were made by a dinosaur walking across mud. The footprints then hardened and were covered with more mud.

Leaf

Fossils of leaves of plants and trees have been found dating back hundreds of millions of years. They can tell us much about the climate.

Fossils in fossils

Fossilized tree resin, called amber, has been found with insects and even small animals, such as frogs, trapped inside and fossilized.

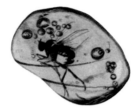

Dinosaur fossils

Entire fossil dinosaur skeletons have been found, but these are very rare. Individual fossilized bones are more common.

Plant pollen

Pollen particles from trees and plants can be preserved for thousands of years. They can tell us about the sort of food our ancestors ate.

Plant pollen magnified hundreds of times

Pompeii casts

Victims of the volcanic eruption of Mount Vesuvius were buried by ash. Their bodies decayed, but plaster casts have been made of the spaces left.

FOSSIL TOOLS

The fossil remains of early humans dating back 400,000 years have been found in a cave at Zhoukoudian near Beijing in China.

Scientists have also found some fossils of the tools they made, such as this deer skull cup.

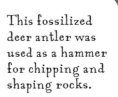

This fossilized deer antler was used as a hammer for chipping and shaping rocks.

Dinosaur bird

The 150 million-year-old fossil of a dinosaur with feathers was discovered in 1861. It gives clues about the link between dinosaurs and birds.

Human ancestors

The fossil bones of some of our earliest ancestors have been found. Scientists have used them to work out what early people looked like.

This is a view of Whitepark
Bay in Northern Ireland,
where the sea is gradually
breaking down the rocks
and cliffs.

Rock collecting

In this section of the book, you'll find helpful information on starting a collection of rocks, minerals or fossils. It shows the kind of equipment you will need on a collecting trip, and how to prepare and take care of your specimens once they're back home.

Starting a collection

Looking for rocks, minerals and fossils can be
great fun, and it's also a good way of learning
about the natural world. But before you go
out collecting, there are some rules you
should always try to follow.

The collectors' code

Always check with the local tourist office
before removing any rocks or fossils,
especially from beaches. Remember that
animals often live underneath rocks, so you
might be disturbing their homes.
　　Rocks help to keep soil and sand in place,
so only take what you need. If too many
rocks are removed by collectors, beaches
and hillsides can be opened up to erosion
from the sea, wind and rain.

On a beach like this, under chalk
cliffs, you're most likely to find
rounded lumps of flint rocks.

What, when and where?

If you take a notebook and pens, you'll be able to record your discoveries. Try to describe all the material you have collected as clearly as possible, including where you found the samples and the date of discovery.

When you are back home, you can refer back to your notes as you are listing your collection. The more information you have, the clearer the picture you'll be able to build up about the rocks, minerals or fossils in your collection, what they are and where they're from.

Open the day's collecting with details of when and where your expedition took place.

Photos and sketches of the area you visited can help you to identify the rocks you found.

Gurgle beach

Bird's eye view of area I visited

Rock sketch

JULY 5th IN GURGLE BAY NEAR ROCKPORT - NICE WARM DRY DAY

COLLECTION	WHERE?	HOW MANY?
Rocks	beach/rockpool	5
Fossils	near cliff	1
Minerals?	couldn't find any!	0

OBSERVATIONS:
The beach sand was dark and fine. This could indicate that it was formed from volcanic rock. Does this fit in with the rest of the information in this area? Good selection of pebbles, various sizes.

You could stick in sand or small pebble samples.

Jot down any points you think may give you more clues about the identity of your samples.

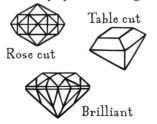
Preparing your collection

It shouldn't be too difficult to build up a good collection of different stones. On many pebble beaches, for example, you can find hard quartzes, such as flint, chalcedony, agate, rose quartz and smoky quartz. They may look dull and uninteresting when you first pick them up, but there's a lot you can do to bring them to life. This is when some of the most interesting work begins.

Polishing stones

To see the full beauty of your stones and their patterns and shades, it helps to polish and varnish them.

You can polish stones by hand using sandpaper. But, to get the best results, you can use a tumble polisher. This is a machine with a rotating drum in which you place your pebbles, a grinding grit and some water.

This is what some common pebbles look like before and after polishing. You can find these on many beaches.

Amethyst

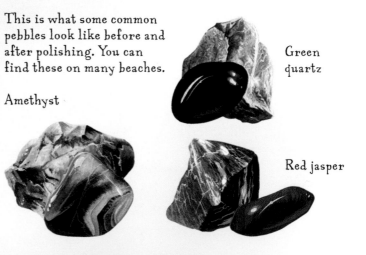

Green quartz

Red jasper

Polished stones can reveal all sorts of interesting lines and patterns.

On display

You can buy special display cabinets with glass shelves to show off your collection – or you could try making a simple wooden display cabinet yourself.

Fragile, delicate specimens should be wrapped with paper or cotton padding to prevent chipping. If you have a friend who's also a rock collector, you may be able to exchange any duplicates in your collection for other specimens you don't have.

PEBBLE JEWELS

You can buy simple metal fittings from hobby shops to turn your best polished stones into rings, brooches, cufflinks and necklaces.

Wooden display cabinet with labelled specimens

(15) Malachite

Shade : Green
Streak : Pale green
Crystal system: Monoclinic

Found: Cornwall, June 12th 08
Recorded : July 29th 08

If your collection grows to hundreds of specimens, it's important to have a clear recording system – or it can become confusing.

When cleaning up your fossils, always chip away from your specimen. In that way, only the unwanted rock will be scratched if your hand slips.

Tap away from the fossil.

Chisel

Collecting fossils

When you are on a fossil hunting expedition, there are two important guidelines to follow.

If you want to remove a fossil from a rock, look closely at the stone to calculate where it will crack. This is so you know the best place to hit it without damaging the fossil.

When you've knocked off the piece of rock with its fossil, wait until you've taken it back home before you chip away at it to tidy it up. Good fossils can be ruined by impatience. Wrap it up in some newspaper to protect it.

Cleaning them

Back home, you'll have plenty of time to work on your new fossil finds. If you can clamp your fossils to a wooden board, it'll make the job of cleaning them much easier.

This ammonite fossil has been tidied up to reveal its patterns. But it has been left on a base of the original rock it was found in.

Making your own fossils

You could make your own fossil imprint and cast. You'll need: a sheet of card, model clay, petroleum jelly, a rolling pin, an object such as a shell or leaf, plaster of Paris, a strip of thin card 5cm (2in) wide and a paperclip.

Many model shops sell rubber latex kits. With this method you can make as many copies of your fossils as you like. Try painting them to give away as presents.

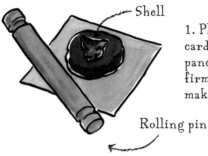

Shell

Rolling pin

1. Place the clay on the card and roll it into a thick pancake. Press your object firmly in the middle to make a clear impression.

1. Paint several layers of latex on your fossil sample, allowing each layer to dry before applying the next.

2. Remove the object and you will be left with its imprint. Now rub petroleum jelly on the surface of the clay.

Petroleum jelly

2. When the last layer is dry, slit the back of it with a sharp knife and peel it off the fossil.

Be very careful!

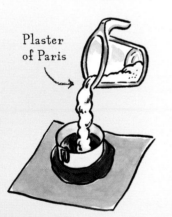

Plaster of Paris

3. Make a collar from the strip of card. Fit it around the imprint, and fasten with paperclip. Mix the plaster of Paris, and pour onto the imprint. Leave it to set hard.

3. Spoon some plaster of Paris into the latex shape until it is full. When set, pop the plaster shape out.

4. Once it has set, after a few hours, remove the collar and pull the plaster away from the clay. You'll be left with an imprint and a cast.

Imprint   Cast

Glossary

Here are some of the words in the book you might not know. Any word in *italics* is defined elsewhere in the glossary.

alloy A mixture of two or more metals, or a metal and a non-metal.

amber A yellow fossil resin from *extinct* coniferous trees.

climate change The change in the world's weather conditions.

continental crust The part of the Earth's *crust* which forms areas of land. It is made mostly of granite rock.

core The central part of the inside of the Earth, which scientists think is made of iron and nickel.

crust The Earth's solid outer layer. It consists of *continental crust* which forms the land, and *oceanic crust* which forms the seabed.

crystal A solid substance, such as quartz, with a regular geometrical shape, in which flat surfaces meet at definite angles.

element A substance that contains only one kind of atom. It cannot be broken down into a simpler form.

era A clearly defined period of time.

extinct An animal or plant species that has died out.

field guide A book for identifying rocks, *minerals* and fossils.

fold mountains A mountain range formed by the Earth's *crust* buckling up into folds when the *plates* of the *crust* push together.

gemstone A decorative *mineral* or organic (living) substance prized for its beauty, rarity and durability.

geode A cavity within a rock that is lined with *crystals*.

geological hammer A hammer specially designed for removing rocks and fossils. It usually has a square head and a chisel edge for splitting rocks.

geology The study of the Earth's rocks and *minerals* and the way they have developed.

glacier A large mass or river of slow-moving ice.

gravel A mixture of rock fragments and pebbles that is coarser than sand.

hot spring A place where hot water, heated by underground rocks, comes to the surface. Also known as a thermal spring.

igneous Igneous rocks are formed when *magma* escapes from inside the Earth, cools and then hardens.

lava Hot *molten magma* that bursts or flows out of *volcanoes* onto the land.

magma Hot, melted rock inside the Earth.

mantle The thick layer of rock under the Earth's *crust*. Some of the rock is solid and some *molten*.

metamorphic Metamorphic rocks are rocks that have been changed by heat or pressure, sometimes both.

meteorite A rock-like object from another planet that has landed on Earth.

microfossil A fossil that is too small to be studied without using a microscope.

These amethyst crystals formed inside a hollow basalt geode.

mineral A non-living substance found in the Earth, such as salt, iron, diamond or quartz. Most rocks are made up of a mixture of minerals.

molten Liquified or melted.

national park A reserve of land, usually owned by a national government, and protected from most human development.

oceanic crust The parts of the Earth's *crust* which form the seabed. Made mostly of basalt rock.

This large group of scallop shells were fossilized in limestone.

oceanic trench A deep trench in the seabed that forms where one *plate* pushes underneath another.

Olduvai Gorge A gorge in Tanzania, East Africa, famous as a site where the fossilized remains of early people have been found.

Pangaea The name given to a huge continent scientists think once existed on Earth. It broke up to form the continents we have today.

plaster of Paris A white powder made from gypsum that sets hard when mixed with water. Used to make sculptures and casts.

plates The separate pieces of *crust* that fit together to cover the Earth.

precious stone A *mineral* of exceptional beauty and rarity often used in jewels.

radioactive decay The process of decay of certain *elements*. As they decay, they give off energy and radiation. The rate of decay can be measured to indicate the age of material such as rock.

sea stack A steep rock in the sea near a coastline. Formed when part of a headland is worn away by the sea.

sedimentary Rock made up of particles of sand, mud and other sediments that have settled on the seabed and been squashed down to form hard rock.

semi-precious stone A *gemstone* that is considered less rare and valuable than a *precious stone*.

smelting The process of extracting a metal from its ore by heating the ore to a high temperature.

stromatolites Simple organisms that have lived from over 3,000 million years ago to the present day.

synthetic gemstone A *gemstone* made artificially by chemical means.

volcano An opening in the Earth's *crust* from which *molten lava*, rock fragments, ash, dust and gases are forced out from below the Earth's surface.

weathering The breakdown of rocks by the action of wind, rain, snow, cold and heat.

Index

A

agate, 59, 86
agglomerate, 32
alabaster, 37, 42
alloy, 61, 90
amber, 71, 81
amethyst, 54, 58, 86
ammonite, 66, 70, 75, 79, 88
amphibolite, 41
andesite, 33
Anning, Mary, 78
apatite, 52
Appalachian mountains, 76
aquamarine, 54, 55, 57
arsenopyrite, 62
augite, 52
Ayers Rock, 36

B

baryte, 52
basalt, 31, 33, 51
batholith, 31
belemnite, 78
beryl, 54, 55
birthstones, 54
bivalve, 79
brachiopod, 74, 79
breccia, 37
bryozoan, 75

C

calcite, 35, 51, 53
Caledonian mountains,
   38, 76
carnelian, 55, 59
cast fossil, 68, 89
Cenozoic era, 67
chalcedony, 58, 86
chalcopyrite 61, 63
chalk, 36, 84
chrysoberyl, 57
cinnabar, 43, 62

clay, 11, 36
climate, 76, 77
coal, 37, 70, 71
Coelacanth, 75
conglomerate, 37
continental crust, 24
copper, 60, 61, 63
coral, 56, 70, 74, 75, 78
core, 8, 22
corundum, 54
crinoid, 70, 78
crust, 8, 23, 24
crystals, 46, 48-49

D

diamond, 10, 47, 54, 57
dinosaur, 69, 80, 81
dolerite, 33

E

earthquake, 25
echinoid, 13, 79
element, 10, 46, 48
emerald, 54, 55, 57
extrusive rock, 31

F

feldspar, 10, 39, 50, 53
fish, 68, 78, 79
fission-track dating, 67
flint, 37, 42, 84, 86
fluorite, 52
fold mountains, 25, 38
fossils, 11, 13, 17, 40,
   65-81
fossil fuels, 72

G

gabbro, 33
galena, 61, 63
garnet, 51, 54, 59
garnet schist, 41

gas, 72
gastropod, 71, 79
geode, 46, 91
geologist, 9, 10, 23, 47,
   48
gemstone, 51, 54-59
Giant's Causeway, 31
glacier, 17, 27
gneiss, 40, 51
gold, 10, 60, 63
Grand Canyon, 35
granite, 10, 15, 18, 30,
   32, 42
gypsum, 37, 51, 53

H

halite 49, 51, 52
hematite, 47, 60, 61, 63
Himalayas, 25
hornblende, 53
hot springs, 31, 91

I

igneous rock, 10, 13, 15,
   30-33, 50
imprint fossil, 68, 89
intrusive rock, 30
iron, 60, 61

J

jade, 55
jadeite, 59
jasper, 86

K

kaolin, 36
karst, 35
Kilauea, 23
kimberlite, 47

L

laccolith, 31
lapis lazuli, 43, 55, 58
Lascaux, 43
lava, 20, 31
lead, 61
limestone, 34, 35, 36, 39, 42, 43

M

magma, 10, 25, 30, 50
magnetite, 63
malachite, 43, 63, 87
mantle, 8, 22, 23, 24, 27
marble, 39, 40, 42
Mesozoic era, 67
metals, 60-63
metamorphic rock, 10, 13, 38-41, 51
meteorite, 9
mica, 10, 39, 41, 50, 53
microfossil, 73, 77, 91
migmatite, 41
milky quartz, 53
minerals, 10, 11, 13, 45-63
Moon, 50, 52
mountains, 15, 25, 26, 76
Mount Fuji, 30
mudstone, 37

N

native element, 47
nature reserve, 85
nautiloid, 74
nephrite, 59

O

obsidian, 33
oceanic crust, 24
oil, 72-73
Olduvai Gorge, 67, 92
olivine, 53

oolite, 37
opal, 54, 56
ore, 60-63
orpiment, 62

P

palaeontologist, 68, 75
Paleozoic era, 67
Pangaea, 76
pebbles, 16, 40, 86, 87
pegmatite, 10, 33
peridot, 54, 57
peridotite, 32
phyllite, 41
plates, 24-25, 77
platinum, 61
potassium-argon dating, 67
Precambrian era, 67
precious metals, 61
precious stones, 54-57
pumice, 23, 33
pyrite, 63

Q

quartz 10, 16, 39, 44, 50, 52, 60, 86
quartzite, 38, 39, 41

R

radioactive decay, 67, 92
rhodonite, 59
rhyolite, 32
ridges, 25
rock crystal, 53
rocks, 7-19, 28-43, 83-89
ruby, 54, 56

S

salt, 46, 49
sand, 11, 16
sandstone, 10, 18, 34, 36, 39, 70

sapphire, 54, 56
schist, 10, 41, 51
sea lily, 71, 74, 78
sea stack, 17, 27, 92
sediment, 10, 11, 27, 34, 35, 66
sedimentary rock, 10, 13, 17, 34-37, 67, 70, 72
semi-precious stones, 55, 58
shale, 37, 71
silicate, 52
silver, 61
slate, 18, 41
smelting, 62, 92
soils, 14, 19, 32
spinel, 56
stalactite, 11, 37
starfish, 75, 79
steel, 61, 63
strata, 67
streak test, 47

T

tools, 42
trace fossil, 66, 79
trilobite, 67, 74, 79
tumble polisher, 86
turquoise, 51, 54, 55, 59

U

Uluru, 36

V

volcano, 8, 23, 31

W

weathering, 26-27, 51
wood fossils, 80

Z

Zhoukoudian, 81
zircon, 57

Acknowledgements

Every effort has been made to trace the copyright holders of material in this book. If any rights have been omitted, the publishers offer to rectify this in any subsequent editions following notification. The publishers are grateful to the following organizations and individuals for their permission to reproduce material

(t = top, m = middle, b = bottom, l = left, r = right):

Cover © Sinclair Stammers/Science Photo Library; **p1** © nagelestock.com/Alamy; **p2–3** © Gavin Kingcome/Science Photo Library; **p4** © Visuals Unlimited/Corbis; **p6–7** © Phil McDermott/Alamy; **p8–9** © Ashley Cooper/Corbis; **p10** (t) © studiomode/Alamy; **p11** (t) © Elvele Images/Alamy; (b) © Herve Conge ISM/Science Photo Library; **p13** (m) © Martin Land/Science Photo Library; **p20-21** © Douglas Peebles/Corbis; **p22-23** © Mauritius/Superstock; **p24-25** (t) © AM Corporation/Alamy; **p28-29** © Tom Bean/Corbis; **p30** (b) © Peter Horree/Alamy; **p31** (t) © Rough Guides/Alamy; **p33** (bl) © United States Geological Survey; (mr) © Dr Richard Busch; **p34** (b) © DEA/L. Romano/De Agostini Picture Library/Getty Images; **p35** (br) © Andy Sotiriou/Digital Vision/Getty Images; **p36** (b) © David Wall/Alamy; **p37** (bl) © United States Geological Survey; (br) © Dave Dyet; **p38** (b) © Tom Bean/Corbis; **p39** (tr) © AAA Photostock/Alamy; **p40** (bl) © David Ball/Alamy; **p41** (m) © Dave Dyet; **p42** (br) © The Natural History Museum/Alamy; **p43** (b) © Richard Murphy/Alamy; **p44-45** © Dirk Wiersma/Science Photo Library; **p46** (b) © Maurice Nimmo, Frank Lane Picture Agency/Corbis; **p47** (t) © E.R. Degginger/Alamy; (ml) © Steve Hamblin/Alamy; **p48** (b) © Lawrence Lawry/Science Photo Library; **p49** (br) © Kari Marttila/Alamy; **p50** (b) © Sebastien Baussais/Alamy; **p51** (tr) © crystalclassics.co.uk; (bl) © Dave Dyet; **p52** (m) © United States Geological Survey; **p53** (tl, m) © United States Geological Survey; **p54** (l) © JewelryStock/Alamy; (b) © Christies Images/Corbis; **p55** (t) © Wildlife GmbH/Alamy; **p56** (m) © GC Minerals/Alamy; (br) © Photodisc/Alamy; **p57** (tl) © Steve Hamblin/Alamy; (tl) © crystalclassics.co.uk; (tm) © Jewellery Specialist/Alamy; (tr) © crystalclassics.co.uk; (bl) © Jewellery Specialist/Alamy; (bm, br) © The Natural History Museum/Alamy; (mr) © Smithsonian Institution/Corbis; **p59** (tr) © Chris Ralph/Nevada-outback-gems.com; (ml) © The Natural History Museum/Alamy; (mr) © United States Geological Survey; (bl) © Maurice Nimmo, Frank Lane Picture Agency/Corbis; (bm) © Dave Dyet; **p60** (bl) © Layne Kennedy/Corbis; (m) © Peter Horree/Alamy; **p61** (b) © Ria Novosti/Science Photo Library; **p62** (m, bm, br) © United States Geological Survey; **p63** (tl, tr) © United States Geological Survey; **p64-65** © Chris Howes/Wild Places Photography/Alamy; **p68** (b) © David R. Frazier Photolibrary Inc./Alamy; **p69** © Ken Lucas/Ardea.com; **p72** (m) © United States Geological Survey; **p73** (tr) © Darlyne A. Murawski/Still Pictures; (b) © Robert Harding Picture Library/Alamy; **p76** (m) © Digital Vision; **p77** (tr) © ISM/Oxford Scientific; **p80** (bl) © John Cancalosi/naturepl.com; **p82-83** © NTPL/Joe Cornish; **p84** © NTPL/Derek Croucher; **p85** (ml) © Digital Vision; **p87** (t) © VStock/Alamy; **p88** (bl) © blickwinkel/Alamy; **p90-91** © PjrFoto studio/Alamy; **p92-93** © John Cancalosi/Alamy.

With thanks to Mike Freeman
Additional designs by Marc Maynard and Karen Tomlins
Cover design by Joanne Kirkby
Digital manipulation by Keith Furnival

Additional illustrations by John Barber, Joyce Bee, Trevor Boyer, Hilary Burn, Kuo Kang Chen, Aziz Khan, Tim Hayward, Alan Male, Andy Martin, Annabel Milne, David Palmer, Julie Piper, Chris Shields, Peter Stebbing, Phil Weire and others